Essays from the Margins

ESSAYS
FROM THE MARGINS

Luis N. Rivera-Pagán

CASCADE *Books* • Eugene, Oregon

ESSAYS FROM THE MARGINS

Copyright © 2014 Luis N. Rivera-Pagán. All rights reserved. Except for brief quotations in critical publications or reviews, no part of this book may be reproduced in any manner without prior written permission from the publisher. Write: Permissions. Wipf and Stock Publishers, 199 W. 8th Ave., Suite 3, Eugene, OR 97401.

Cascade Books
An Imprint of Wipf and Stock Publishers
199 W. 8th Ave., Suite 3
Eugene, OR 97401

www.wipfandstock.com

ISBN 13: 978-1-62564-604-0

Cataloguing-in-Publication Data

Rivera Pagán, Luis.

    Essays from the margins / by Luis N. Rivera-Pagán.

    x + 152 pp. ; 23 cm. Includes bibliographical references.

    ISBN 13: 978-1-62564-604-0

    1. Theology—Latin America. 2. Bible—Hermeneutics—Comparative studies. 3. Christianity and politics. 4. Liberation theology. 5. Palestine—In Christianity. I. Title.

BT83.57 .R58 2014

Manufactured in the U.S.A.   11/17/2014

In homage to George V. Pixley, in the 1960s my first professor of biblical studies, in the 1970s my faculty colleague, and, for the last fifty years, my dear friend. During his many years of teaching at Puerto Rico's Seminario Evangélico, México's Comunidad Teológica, Nicaragua's Seminario Bautista, and lecturing all over Latin America, George Pixley inspired myriad students to do their best, as members of the academy, society, and church. He has written many books and numberless essays in Spanish and English, several of them translated into Portuguese, forging a particular and unique convergence between the most rigorously critical biblical hermeneutics, the emerging and exciting liberation theologies, and process philosophy.

Contents

Preface | ix

1 **A Prophetic Challenge to the Church**
   The Last Word of Bartolomé de las Casas | 1

2 **A View from Below**
   Female Lament and Defiance in Times of War | 27

3 **Listening and Engaging the Voices from the Margins**
   Postcolonial Observations from the Caribbean | 44

4 **God the Liberator**
   Theology, History, and Politics | 63

5 **Xenophilia or Xenophobia**
   Towards a Theology of Migration | 84

6 **Reading the Hebrew Bible in Solidarity with the Palestinian People** | 104

Bibliography | 131

Preface

We are a small and lonely human race
Showing no sign of mastering solitude
Out on this stony planet that we farm.
The most that we can do for one another
Is let our blunders and our blind mischances
Argue a certain brusque abrupt compassion.
We might as well be truthful.

—ADRIENNE RICH[1]

The poetic requirements enunciated by Adrienne Rich in this verse, published when she was still a young writer trying to find and forge her own literary voice—to merge "brusque abrupt compassion" with the will to "be truthful"—have their peculiar existential and theological dimensions. Rich was clearly aware what they meant for her as a poet, woman, feminist, anti-war activist, and a believer in the equality of all human beings despite their differences in gender, race, national origin, cultural identity, or sexual orientation. And she was indeed willing to pay the price and to endure the sacrifices entailed. Whether she was also conscious of any religious or theological implications, I leave it to the literary critics interested in analyzing her poetic heritage.

This challenge—to forge a close link between a "brusque abrupt compassion" and the will to "be truthful"—happens to be the hidden inspiration of the lectures and essays reproduced in this book. These essays emerge from different crucial and complex conflicts. From the memory of

1. "Stepping Backward," in *Poems*, 8.

Preface

a bishop, Bartolomé de las Casas, urging the Pope of his time to cleanse the church from complicity with violence, oppression, and slavery; from the lament and defiance of so many Middle East women, victims of male domination and so many wars; from the voices bursting out from the colonial margins that dare to question and transgress the norms and laws imposed by colonizers and conquerors; from the emerging and diverse theological disruptions of traditional orthodoxies and rigid dogmatisms; from the denial of human rights to immigrant communities, living in the shadows of opulent societies, by those always so proud of their exclusive civil rights; from the use of the Hebrew sacred scriptures to displace and dispossess the indigenous peoples of Palestine.

They belong to different intellectual genres and conceptual crossroads and are thus illustrative of the dialogic imagination that the Russian intellectual Mikhail Bakhtin considered basic to any serious intellectual enterprise.[2] Yet, they have a hidden connection - the linkage of the "brusque abrupt compassion" and the will to "be truthful," above mentioned. These essays are also the literary sediment of years of sharing lectures, dialogues, and debates in several academic institutions in the United States, Mexico, Argentina, Chile, Costa Rica, Malaysia, Switzerland, Germany, and Palestine. They are here published with the sole objective of inspiring new dialogues and debates, nurtured by the dialectics of compassion and truthfulness.

This book is dedicated to a person close to my heart and mind: George V. Pixley, who in the 1960s was my professor of biblical studies, in the 1970s my faculty colleague, and, for the last fifty years, my dear friend. During his many years of teaching and lecturing all over Latin America, George Pixley inspired myriad students to do their best, as members of the academy, society and church. He has written many books and numberless essays in Spanish and English, several of them translated into Portuguese, forging a particular and unique convergence between the most rigorously critical biblical hermeneutics, the emerging liberation theologies, and process philosophy.

---

2. Bakhtin, *Dialogic Imagination*.

1

A Prophetic Challenge to the Church
The Last Word of Bartolomé de las Casas[1]

We were always loyal to lost causes . . . Success is for us the death of the intellect and of the imagination.

—JAMES JOYCE[2]

Perhaps there is a dignity in defeat that hardly belongs to victory.

—JORGE LUIS BORGES[3]

To see the possibility, the certainty, of ruin, even at the moment of creation; it was my temperament.

—V. S. NAIPAUL[4]

WHEN THINGS FALL APART

In 1566, after more than five decades of immense and exhausting endeavors to influence and shape the policy of the Spanish state and church regarding

1. Inaugural lecture as the Henry Winters Luce Professor in Ecumenics and Mission of Princeton Theological Seminary, delivered on April 9, 2003.
2. Joyce, *Ulysses*, 131.
3. Borges, *This Craft of Verse*, 45.
4. Naipaul, *Enigma of Arrival*, 52.

the Americas, years of drafting countless historical texts, theological treatises, colonization projects, prophetic homilies, juridical complaints, political utopias, and even apocalyptic visions, Bartolomé de las Casas knows very well that the end is at hand: the end of his life[5] and the end of his illusions of crafting a just and Christian empire in the New World.[6] It is a moment of searching for the precise closure, the right culmination and consummation of a human existence that since 1502 had been intimately linked, as no other person of his time, to the drama of the conquest and Christianization of Latin America, a continent, as has been so aptly asserted, "born in blood and fire."[7]

He painfully knows that there will be no time to finish his *opus magnum*, the *History of the Indies*. Originally conceived as six volumes, each one intended to cover a decade between 1490 and 1550, it will be left partially written, with only the first three decades discussed. In his will, Las Casas makes provision for the preservation of that precious manuscript on which he has worked incessantly for almost forty years. It will survive as a clandestine subversive text for three centuries,[8] will not be published until the second half of the nineteenth century,[9] only very recently has been the object of a truly scholar critical edition,[10] and still lacks a complete and adequate English translation.[11]

5. There is a convenient edition of Las Casas's writings, *Obras completas*, in 14 volumes (1988–1998), published under the supervision of the Spanish scholar Paulino Castañeda Delgado. The secondary bibliography is immense. Essential works are the following: Giménez Fernández, *Bartolomé de las Casas, Vol. I: Delegado de Cisneros para la reformación de las Indias*; Giménez Fernández, *Bartolomé de las Casas, Vol. II: Capellán de Carlos I, poblador de Cumaná*; Pérez Fernández, *Inventario documentado de los escritos de Fray Bartolomé de las Casas*; Pérez Fernández, *Cronología documentada de los viajes, estancias y actuaciones de Fray Bartolomé de las Casas*, Gutiérrez; *Las Casas: In Search of the Poor of Jesus Christ*; and Bataillon *Études sur Bartolomé de las Casas*.

6. A suggestive analysis of the inner conflicts and ambiguities of Las Casas's concept of a Christian and just empire in the New World is provided by Capdevila, *Las Casas, une politique de l'humanité*.

7. Chasteen, *Born in Blood and Fire*.

8. Philip II ordered the confiscation of Las Casas's writings, after the bishop's death, according to Rosner, *Missionare und Musketen*, 212.

9. Spain's Real Academia de la Historia decided to publish it in 1821, a project that immediately reawakened such a heated controversy and offended the national pride of so many Spaniards that its fulfillment had to wait until 1875–1876, when it was printed in five volumes.

10. *Historia de las Indias* (primera edición crítica), in Las Casas, *Obras completas*, volumes 3–5.

11. There is an incomplete English translation: Las Casas, *History of the Indies*, a

A Prophetic Challenge to the Church

In the prologue to the *History of the Indies*, drafted apparently in 1552, Las Casas reveals the diverse objectives of the book:

- To call the attention of the readers to the terrifying disparity between the missionary purpose of the encounter between Christian Europeans and Native Americans and the brutal exploitation of the second by the first.
- To refute the, in his views, many mistakes and deceptions written by other Spanish historians, like Gonzalo Fernández de Oviedo y Valdés[12] and Francisco López de Gómara,[13] who, according to Las Casas, confuse and conflate historiography with sycophancy.
- To proclaim the humanity of the indigenous peoples, their rationality, their personal and collective freedom. "All peoples are human," is the leitmotiv and guiding principle of the text.
- To record a dissenting testimony with the hope that his *History* will one day be read, by future generations, or even maybe at the eschatological moment of reckoning in which his nation, Spain, might hear, with fear and trembling, the fateful hymn—*dies irae, dies illa, solvet saeclum in favilla* . . .
- To ease his profound agony of witnessing a tragic performance of human cruelty, to exorcise the stain of complicity in the atrocities performed.

The *History* is a splendid expression of a passionate obsession, similar to that expressed in Coleridge's famous verse,

> Since then, at an uncertain hour,
> That agony returns,
> And till my ghastly tale is told,
> This heart within me burns.[14]

The *History* would not be a totally forgotten text. Several chroniclers of the Iberian expansion in the Americas would use it as a source for their own books.[15] It became indispensable for all studies on the early encounters

---

rather unsatisfactory rendering of this important work.

12. Oviedo y Valdés, *Historia general y natural de las Indias*.

13. López de Gómara, *Historia general de las indias*.

14. "The Rime of the Ancient Mariner" (II, 582–585), in *Complete Poetical Works of Samuel Taylor Coleridge*, 208.

15. E.g., Herrera y Tordesillas, *Historia general de los hechos de los castellanos en las islas y tierra firme del Mar Océano* (1601–1605) and Remesal, *Historia general de las*

between Europeans and Native Americans, for it contains long and detailed extracts from Christopher Columbus's lost notes and journals regarding his transatlantic expeditions. In fact, all editions of the so-called Diary of Columbus's first journey (1492–1493) derive directly from Las Casas's *History*.[16]

It also became a crucial source for the cognition of many contemporary events, of greater or lesser importance. The *History* contains the first recorded homily in the Americas, an earth shaking sermon preached by the Dominican friar Antonio de Montesinos, the fourth Sunday of Advent of 1511 in which this ardent priest, after reading the biblical passage of John the Baptist, *ego vox clamantis in deserto* (Matt 3:3), preaches these scathing words to the leaders of the Spanish colonial establishment:

> You are in mortal sin . . . for the cruelty and tyranny you use in dealing with these innocent people. Tell me, by what right or justice do you keep these Indians in such a cruel and horrible servitude? On what authority have you waged a detestable war against these people? . . . Why do you keep them so oppressed? . . . Are not these people also human beings? . . . Be certain that in such a state as this you can be no more saved than a Moor or a Turk . . .[17]

The *History* is also the source for the fascinating stories regarding the Caribbean cacique Hatuey, leader of the native resistance who preferred to be burned at the stake rather than be baptized and share heaven with the Christians.[18] Las Casas is the original crafter of the legendary image of this tragic and courageous native who chose death rather than submission.

Yet, during his last year of existence, Las Casas fears that his life long struggle may have been fruitless. What had always moved him to write and act was his intense awareness of possessing a unique historical mission; yet this vocation seems to be floundering. Since his first public intervention, a sermon preached the Day of the Assumption of Our Lady, August 15, 1514,[19] till his last writings more than five decades later, he would be pos-

---

Indias Occidentales (1619).

16. See Dunn and Kelley, Jr., *The Diario of Christopher Columbus's First Voyage to America* and the seventh volume of the series *Repertorium Columbianum*, *Las Casas on Columbus*, edited by Nigel Griffin.

17. *Historia de las Indias* [*HI*], l. 3, cs. 3–7, 1757–1774. Lewis Hanke baptised this sermon as "the first cry for justice in America," in his now classic book *Spanish Struggle for Justice in the Conquest of America*, 15–22.

18. *HI*, l. 3, cs. 21 and 25, 1843–1845, 1863–1864.

19. *HI*, l. 3, c. 79, 2080–2085.

sessed by one obsessive passion: to be the prophet of Spain,[20] a man called by God to be the scourge of the conscience of his nation and to be the defender of the autochthonous communities, in whose misery he perceived "Jesus Christ . . . not once, but thousand times whipped, insulted, beaten, and crucified . . ."[21] If his first writings exude enthusiasm and optimism, the time is now at hand to contemplate the tragic fate of historical action. It is the time in which all things seem to fall apart.

It is the time, under the shadow of death, to look back at his life, a life of a man of letters and a man of action, a man of the church and of the people, a priest, a Dominican friar, a theologian, a prophet, and a bishop. The hour comes of final reckoning, in which the past overwhelms the mind with its fateful irreversibility, and the future with the certainty of its dissolution. His was the bitter honor of having many public noisy detractors[22] and many secret silent admirers, ever since that day, half a century earlier, in which he had the enigmatic intuition of being called to a prophetic vocation.[23] For Las Casas, that kairotic occasion was linked to a biblical text: *Ecclesiasticus* 34:20–21.

> To offer a sacrifice from the
> possessions of the poor
> is like killing a son
> before his father's eyes.
> Bread is life to the destitute,
> and to deprive them of it is murder.[24]

---

20. See Pérez Fernández, "El perfil profético del padre Las Casas," 281–359; Pérez Fernández, "La fidelidad del Padre Las Casas a su carisma profético," 65–109; and André-Vincent, "Le prophétisme de Barthélemy de Las Casas," 541–60. Wagner calls Las Casas "the Jeremiah of the Spaniards." Wagner, *Life and Writings of Bartolomé de las Casas*, 242. According to Rosner, Las Casas, in his historical books, "war weniger Chronist als vielmehr prophetischer und theologischer Interpret der Geschichte" (*Missionare und Musketen*, 213).

21. *HI*, l. 3, c. 138, 2366.

22. Toribio de Benavente Motolinia, a Franciscan missionary, in a letter to Charles V, accused Las Casas of national betrayal. The humanist Juan Ginés de Sepúlveda accused him of heresy. The pugnacious bishop survived both indictments. "Carta de Fray Toribio de Motolinia al Emperador Carlos V" (enero 2 de 1555), in *Historia de los indios de la Nueva España*, 203–21. Sepúlveda, "Proposiciones temerarias, escandalosas y heréticas. . .," in Fabié, *Vida y escritos de don Fray Bartolomé de Las Casas*, Vol. II, 543–69.

23. Ramos Pérez, "La 'conversión' de Las Casas en Cuba," 247–57 and García, *La conversion a los indios de Bartolomé de las Casas*.

24. *The Revised English Bible*, section of the Apocrypha, 122. The Latin text used by La Casas is even stronger. "To offer a sacrifice from the possessions of the poor is

As in the most famous case of another Catholic bishop, St. Augustine, the reading of a biblical text, in a rather mysterious way, forged a sense of unique identity, vocation, and mission. It also, as for St. Augustine, shaped a lifetime of ardent disputes and bitter antagonisms.

Under the shadow of death, the awareness of being unable to fulfill one's vocation can be the most shattering human experience. Paradoxically, it could be even more intense if that person has acquired, due to his writings and deeds, prestige. That feeling of utter existential failure is what probably led José María Arguedas, a widely respected Peruvian writer, to leave unfinished, in 1969, what he thought would have been his best literary achievement, the novel *El zorro de arriba y el zorro de abajo*,[25] and choose instead to put an end to his anguished life with his own hands. The same feeling of despondency also impelled Primo Levi, enjoying international acclamation as the most austere and sober witness of the Shoah, to conclude, by his own will, his nightmares of Auschwitz.[26] A similar hopelessness led William Styron, at the height of his reputation as an author, to contemplate with all seriousness suicide as a possible end of his painful spiritual sorrows.[27] There are, indeed, times when, as Jeremiah or Job, one is inclined to lament: "Cursed be the day on which I was born" (Jeremiah 20:14), "let that day be darkness" (Job 3:4), times when, as Yeats wrote:

> Things fall apart; the centre cannot hold
> ... and everywhere
> The ceremony of innocence is drowned ... .[28]

---

like killing a son before his father's eyes" is rendered: *Qui offert sacrificium ex substantia pauperum, quasi qui victimat filium in conspectu patris sui.* The expression *ex substantia pauperum* ("from the substance of the poor") implies that what is taken from the dispossessed is decisive for their existence. The crux of the matter seems to be the life or death of the Native American peoples. Las Casas quotes this text in two slightly different ways in *HI*, l. 1, c. 24, 473, and *HI*, l. 3, c. 79, 2081.

25. Arguedas, *El zorro de arriba y el zorro de abajo* (Enlish translation: *The Fox from Up Above and the Fox from Down Below*). For a discussion of the relationship between Gustavo Gutiérrez, the theologian, and Arguedas, the novelist, see Greider, "Crossing Deep Rivers: The Liberation Theology of Gustavo Gutiérrez in the Light of the Narrative Poetics of José María Arguedas."

26. Kremer, *Memory and Mastery*.

27. Styron, *Darkness Visible*.

28. Yeats, "The Second Coming" (1919/1920), in *The New Oxford Book of English Verse*, 820.

A Prophetic Challenge to the Church

Times when, as Albert Camus wrote, suicide seems to be the most serious philosophical problem.[29]

THE EPISTLE TO THE ROYAL COUNCIL OF INDIES: A CHALLENGE TO THE CROWN

Suicide have I written? That tragic end might be considered by people like Arguedas, Levi, Styron, or Camus. Not, however, by Las Casas. His intense prophetic self-awareness places him in the category of those who, when the final hour comes, go out fighting. Aware of the imminence of his death, he writes two epistles, short and sharp, restating the principles that had guided all his endeavors. These will constitute his last battle cry. One of the letters is to the Royal Council of Indies, the other to the recently elected Pope, Pius V. For a man accustomed to writing compendious, copious, dense and labyrinthine texts, they are surprisingly, and refreshingly, brief, clear, and precise. Both are important letters, drafted in an era in which the writing of epistles was an exquisite literary art.[30]

This essay is mainly devoted to the epistle to the Pope, but we should not lose sight of the fact that in Las Casas's mind both texts belong together, as his last word to the state and the church regarding a matter that he considers of the most importance for the future of the Christian faith and of humanity. More significant, in his view, than the controversy then acrimoniously dividing Western Christendom: the Protestant Reformation and the Council of Trent.[31]

The tone of his farewell letter to the Council is sharp and blunt.[32] The old bishop, of more than eighty years of age, refuses to mellow. Las Casas

---

29. *Le mythe de Sisyphe*, 15: "Il n'y a qu'un problème philosophique vraiment sérieux: c'est le suicide."

30. I have discussed the fascinating linkage between worldly curiosity and the epistle as a literary genre in the fifteenth and sixteenth centuries in an essay on Columbus's famous 1493 letter to Luis de Santangel. See "Paradise Found: Columbus's Rhetoric of Possession," in Rivera-Pagán, *Essays From the Diaspora*, 37–59.

31. Which of the two letters was written before the other is of interest for a detailed chronology of Las Casas's life, but it is methodologically preferable to see both texts as conjoined expressions of his intention of uttering his final prophetic and theological word. Pérez de Tudela believes the Council of Indies letter to be from 1565. *Obras escogidas de Fray Bartolomé de las Casas*, Vol. V, 536–538. Pérez Fernández, the most important contemporary student of Las Casas, considers it to have been written and sent in 1566. *Inventario documentado de los escritos*, 779–92.

32. Reproduced as appendix in Las Casas, *De regia potestate*, 282–83.

becomes an Iberian Jeremiah confronting the unfaithful king of Judah. The document reiterates what he has been proclaiming during five decades. It emphasizes the missionary purpose of the Spanish dominion of the New World, excoriates the Spanish conquest and enslavement of the indigenous communities, calls for a radical change in the colonial policy, defends his ministry as protector of the Native Americans, proclaims the sacramental obligation of restitution as a requirement for the divine absolution of Spain's sins, and warns the authorities about an imminent eschatological divine condemnation.

The issues are not only political and economic. For the author, a bishop and theologian, the overarching theme is theological: the tragic history of God's grace and human sinfulness. The whole first book of the *History of the Indies* is guided by two conflicting ideas: First, the encounter between Christian Spaniards and Native Americans was a crucial act in the eschatological redemption of all nations, and as such it was a manifestation of divine grace. Second, Spain, the divinely chosen people, has proven to be as rebellious and sinful as the Old Testament Israel. It might thus be fated to share its same tragic destiny.

Always a man of letters, inclined to the process of dialogue and debate, he suggests that the Council convene a board of the best theologians and jurists to discuss the situation created by the violence, dispossession, and servitude suffered by the Native Americans. He also tells the Council that he has sent to the court two treatises ("tratadillos") that could illuminate and guide the deliberations of that advisory board.[33] At the end of the letter, as a terrifying explosion of a volcano, comes the harsh enumeration of eight conclusions that such a theological and juridical board should discuss:

> First, all the wars usually called conquests were and are unjust and tyrannical.
>
> Second, we have illegally usurped all the kingdoms of the Indies.
>
> Third, all encomiendas are iniquitous and tyrannical.
>
> Fourth, those who posses them and those who distribute them are in mortal sin.
>
> Fifth, the king has no more right to justify the conquests and encomiendas than the Ottoman Turk to make war against Christians.

---

33. Apparently he refers to *De Thesauris in Peru* (in Latin) and *El tratado de las doce dudas* (in Spanish), written two or three years before and dedicated to Philip II. Published in *Obras completas*, Vols. 11.1 and 11.2, respectively.

A Prophetic Challenge to the Church

Sixth, all fortunes made in the Indies are to be considered as stolen.

Seventh, if the guilty of complicity in the conquests or encomiendas do not make restitution, they will not be saved.

Eighth, the Indian nations have the right, which will be theirs till the Day of Judgment, to make just war against us and erase us from the face of the earth.[34]

There is in this letter, as in his will, drafted in 1564, a sense of urgency, for who knows with certainty when the final Day of Judgment will occur? There is, in these last writings, an awareness of the proximity not only of his own individual death, but also something like the intuition, shared by several of his contemporaries,[35] that the end of all times, the consummation, both hoped and dreaded, of human history might be at hand. Las Casas fears that it might be a day of condemnation and punishment for his own nation, Spain. "A day," as he writes in his will, "in which God will pour his indignation and anger over Spain, for she has all, in greater or lesser degree, participated in the bloody riches stolen and illicitly acquired, and in the massacres and violence suffered by the Native Americans."[36]

The acts of the Council solemnly note that the letter was respectfully read, heard, and . . . filed.[37]

---

34. The eighth conclusion indicates a key difference between Francisco de Vitoria and Las Casas. Whereas Vitoria analyzes the justice of the Spanish wars against the Native Americans, Las Casas explains why the wars of the Native Americans against the Spaniard are just.

35. Phelan, *Millennial Kingdom of the Franciscans in the New World*. For a brief synopsis of the growth and ebb of apocalyptic urgency in the sixteenth century American missionary enterprise, see Bataillon, "Novo mundo e fim do mundo," 343–51.

36. *Obras escogidas de Fray Bartolomé de las Casas, Vol. V: Opúsculos, cartas y memoriales*, 540.

37. Ibid., 538: ". . . y a esto ninguna cosa proveyeron" ("regarding this petition, they did not take any action") is the austere testimony of Alonso de la Veracruz, an Augustinian friar who, accompanied by two Dominican friars, members of the small coterie of devout followers of Las Casas, read the letter to the Council, in representation of the ailing bishop. The attempts of some Spanish scholars to demonstrate a positive reaction from the authorities to Las Casas's demands might be understandable nationalism, but miss the heart of the confrontation. Las Casas was requesting something that the Council of Indies was constitutionally unable to concede: to declare illegal and illegitimate the Spanish dominion of America as it had historically taken place.

Essays from the Margins

THE LETTER TO THE POPE: A CHALLENGE TO THE CHURCH

For a Roman Catholic bishop to write a letter to the Pope seems initially neither surprising nor illicit. In sixteenth-century Spain, it could be both.

Early in that century, the crown had been able to exact from Rome extensive regulatory formal authority over the church in the Americas. The *Patronato Real* (Royal Patronage), based upon several Papal decrees enacted under the relentless pressure of Ferdinand V, gave the crown ample powers over the demarcation, administration, and finances of the American dioceses, including the nomination of bishops.[38] Ferdinand, Charles V and Philip II will consider those Papal documents—Alexander VI's 1493 bulls *Inter caetera* and *Eximiae devotionis*, his 1501 bull *Eximiae devotionis*, and Julius II's 1508 bull *Universalis ecclesiae*—as the juridical foundation of their royal patronage over the American church.[39]

The royal patronage over the American church could even be said to function as a sort of royal vicariate, or at least such was the import of the legislative and juridical actions in ecclesiastical matters undertaken by the court.[40] According to a Spanish scholar, the royal patronage, "created a peculiar situation, extraordinary in canon law, characterized by a transfer to the state of powers and functions traditionally exercised exclusively by the supreme ecclesiastical authority."[41] As the sixteenth century evolved, this peculiar regime in which the crown had assumed, in the words of another scholar, a "quasi-pontifical character,"[42] began to acquire a precise juridical status in the emerging labyrinth of the Laws of Indies, a process that Rome observed with apprehension but also with a good amount of restrictive powerlessness. The law required of all bishops and archbishops, before their entrance into office, to swear fealty to the crown and loyal obedience to the royal patronage. One of its consequences was that controversial matters between church and state, in the Americas, were usually submitted to the crown, rather than to Rome, for a normative resolution.

38. See Leturia, *Relaciones entre la Santa Sede e Hispanoamérica* and Shiels, *King and Church: The Rise and Fall of the Patronato Real*.

39. Reproduced in Shiels, *King and Church*, 283–89, 294–95 and 310–13.

40. *Relaciones*, I, 101–52. See also Gutiérrez de Arce, "Regio patronato indiano (Ensayo de valoración histórico-canónica)," 107–68 and Alberto de la Hera, "El Patronato y el Vicariato Regio en Indias," 63–79.

41. Gutiérrez de Arce, "Regio patronato indiano," 109.

42. Shiels, *King and Church*, 184.

A Prophetic Challenge to the Church

Even when the discursive rhetoric of many formal documents regarding church and state affairs, like the 1493 bulls[43] or the notorious *requerimiento*,[44] emphasized Papal authority, it was eminently clear that the power for historical action was mainly in the hands of the state.[45] The rhetoric might be ultramontane, but the political praxis was strongly royalist. The Burgos capitulations, signed in 1512 by the crown and the first three bishops named to the Americas, was one of the first expressions of that royal patrimony. It is a document with a strong juridical tenor, in which the crown establishes the boundaries of the functions and attributes of the American episcopacy.[46] For the Spanish authorities, the Burgos Capitulations became a paradigm of the powerful jurisdiction to exercise over ecclesiastical affairs in the New World in process of conquest and colonization.[47]

This certainly does not mean that the relations between church and state were devoid of conflicts, or that the Pope always agreed to remain a spectator at the margins of the exceptional historical drama unfolding in the Americas. In 1537, Pope Paul III enacted the bull *Sublimis Deus*, in which he used very strong language calling for the recognition and respect of the humanity and freedom of the autochthonous communities. The Pope also sent a brief to the Archbishop of Toledo, *Pastorale officium*, urging the highest ecclesiastical hierarch of Spain to protect the liberties and rights of the Native Americans.[48] The reaction of the court of Charles V was swift

---

43. Giménez Fernández, *Nuevas consideraciones sobre la historia, sentido y valor de las bulas alejandrinas* and "Algo más sobre las bulas alejandrinas de 1493 referentes a las Indias."

44. For a concise analysis of the origin, evolution, and conflicting evaluations of the *requerimiento*, see Biermann, "Das Requerimiento in der spanischen Conquista." Also Rivera-Pagán, *Violent Evangelism*, 32–41.

45. Alberto de la Hera, "El regalismo indiano," 81–97.

46. Reproduced in Shiels, *King and Church*, 319–25. The signing prelates were Fray García de Padilla, Pedro Suárez de Deza, and Alonso Manso, nominated bishops for the recently created dioceses of Santo Domingo, Concepción de la Vega, and San Juan, respectively.

47. For Las Casas, it became the wrong paradigm, a model of mistaken docility and submissiveness of the church to the state. See Rivera-Pagán, "Las Capitulaciones de Burgos," 33–60 and "Iglesia y colonialidad," 15–45.

48. Helen Rand Parish reproduces the Latin text of the bull and the brief, with a Spanish translation, in *Las Casas en México*, 303–5, 310–12. There are English versions of both documents in Las Casas, *Only Way*, 114–15, 156–57 and in Las Casas, *In Defense of the Indians*, 100–103. In his anthology of ecclesiastical normative documents regarding the Spanish empire, Hernáez reproduces *Pastorale officium*, but not *Sublimis Deus*, though he includes *Veritas ipsa*, a variant of *Sublimis Deus*. He blames Las Casas for the

and energetic, forcing the Pope to retract, in 1538.[49] The traumatic events of the May 1527 sacking of Rome, in which the imperial troops rampaged through the city, looted everything they could, and ignominiously humbled the *Vicarius Christi*, were still painfully fresh in the memory of the Roman authorities and prescribed supreme prudence before engaging in any possible confrontation with the Emperor.

One key dimension of the royal patronage was the *pase regio*, the royal *exequatur* or *placet*. According to it, all communications between Rome and the American church had to be sent first to the Council of Indies for its examination and approval. It was an important strategic resource for the centralizing politics of the Hapsburg monarchy. It was a strategy to impede the emergence, within the ranks of the church, of any serious challenge to the colonial metropolitan policies.[50]

"exaggerated news" regarding the mistreatment of the Native Americans as the source for the Pope's concern and reproduces some of the most denigrating testimonies against the Native Americans ever expressed in the sixteenth century. Hernáez, *Colección de bulas, breves y otros documentos*, Vol. I, 101–4. *Pastorale officium* and *Veritas ipsa*, but not *Sublimis Deus*, are included in Metzler, *America Pontificia. Primi saeculi evangelizationis, 1493–1592*, Vol. I, 359–61, 364–66. For a detailed analysis of these Papal documents, see de la Hera, "El derecho de los indios a la libertad y a la fe: la bula *Sublimis Deus* y los problemas indianos que la motivaron," 89–182. Parish has given a closer look to the origin of these documents, including another 1537 Papal bull, *Altitudo divini consilii*, regarding the perfomance of some sacraments and liturgical ceremonies in the New World (*Las Casas en México*, 15–28, 82–90).

49. The abrogating Papal brief, *Non indecens videtur*, is reproduced, in Latin with a Spanish translation, in Parish's *Las Casas en México*, 313–15. Francisco de Vitoria does not mention *Sublimis Deus* in his 1539 lectures on the Native Americans (*De Indis*, I). Jeremy Lawrance suggests that the lecture might have been inspired by the controversy about the Papal decrees. However, Vitoria deals mainly with matters regarding the justice of the wars against the Native Americans, not their slavery, which is the main theme of the Pope's bull. Vitoria, *Political Writings*, 233 n. 3. Acosta barely alludes to it once in his important 1588 book on the the Christianization of the Americas, *De procuranda indorum salute*, Vol. I, 114. Las Casas, for one, quoted both documents as valid and normative. Probably thanks to his influence many readers tend to disregard their revocation. See Hanke, "Pope Paul III and the American Indians," Vol. 30, 1937, 56–102; Martínez, "Las Casas-Vitoria y la bula *Sublimis Deus*," 25–51; and Gutiérrez, "Las Casas y Paulo III," 33–42.

50. There are conflicting evaluations of the royal patronage. Gutiérrez de Arce considers it a very useful tool to achieve the Christianization of the Americas. Shiels is of the opinion that it "dealt a shattering blow to the independent administrative machinery of the universal church. In fact, it made the Spanish church a state church" (*King and Church*, 192).

A Prophetic Challenge to the Church

Las Casas's letter to Pope Pius V[51] consciously disregards the *pase regio*. The very act of writing to the Pope without previously submitting the text to the Royal Council of Indies violates one of the main juridical premises of the church and state relations in the Americas. It is a transgression of the ecclesiastical policy so carefully crafted by the Spanish court.[52] True to form, even to his last breath, Las Casas would be the perennial dissenter.[53] As bishop of Chiapas, he had imposed a set of norms that rigorously conditioned sacramental absolution of the Spaniards to the restitution of all goods and riches acquired on the basis of conquest or slavery of the Native Americans, a move that forced him to exile from his diocese; as a theologian, he printed and distributed, in 1552, a series of polemic treatises regarding the *status confessionis* in the New World, without requesting any official permission to do so; as a dying prophet he disregards the law of the state and appeals directly to the Pope.

Las Casas begins in a rather professorial tone, devoid of the reverent language so frequent in communications to the successor of saint Peter:

> What things are necessary for the correct way of preaching the Gospel to the infidels, and to render just and legitimate the wars against them, I have declared in the book that I sent to Your Beatitude... To Your Beatitude I beseech intensively, by the blood of our Redemption, to command that my book be examined and, if found right, that it be stamped...

Las Casas holds onto the illusion that reason will, in the end, prevail over irrationality, goodness over evil, grace over sin, if only the main protagonists

---

51. Manuscript in the National Library of Paris, ms. 325, fol. 312. Published for the first time in 1866 in the second volume of the *Colección de documentos para la historia de México*, edited by García Icazbalceta, 599–600. Reproduced in *Obras escogidas, vol. V*, 541–42 and in *Obras completas, vol. 13*, 370–71. English translation in Rivera-Pagán, *Essays From the Diaspora*, 108–10. It is a text neglected by scholars, with the exception of Isacio Pérez Fernández, *Inventario documentado de los escritos*, 762–76. Gutiérrez considers it "a very significant text" (*Las Casas*, 90), without however analyzing it. The manuscript appears to be incomplete, it lacks the introduction and conclusion typical of such epistles. It might be a preliminary draft.

52. Juan Friede rightly stresses the importance of the letter as an act of legal disobedience. But he does not perceive the originality of the challenges that the letter raises to the Roman Church, and not only to the Spanish state. Friede, *Bartolomé de Las Casas: precursor del anticolonialismo*, 214–16.

53. See Rivera-Pagán, "Prophecy and Patriotism: A Tragic Dilemma From the Cross of Terror," 87–101, 315–17 and Rivera-Pagán, "Violence of the Conquistadores and Prophetic Indignation," 37–49, 239–43.

of the historical drama will think things through adequately. He has the hope that, despite all the economic and political interests intertwined in the conquest of the Indies, despite the *conquistadores'* quest for power, profit, and prestige, he might be able to convince the crown, the royal council, and the Pope to follow the right path. Persuasion by means of the right arguments, the quotation of the proper authorities and texts, the coherence of logical reasoning: this is the illusion that has impelled him to write so many books, like his two apologies against Juan Ginés de Sepúlveda in which he buried his adversary, as well as the readers, under a deluge of references, authoritative quotations, and arguments.[54] If only the authorities, those who have the power to make decisions, would read his books and take the time to pay attention to his words![55]

There is no absolute certainty about the book he sent to the Pope whose official approval he is requesting. It might be *De unico vocationis modo omnium gentium ad veram religionem*, a text with a tortuous, and still somewhat obscure, manuscript history.[56] In it, one of the most important missiological books written in the sixteenth century, Las Casas vigorously insists that there is only one way to convert the innumerable gentiles and infidels that the Iberians were encountering in their global expeditions: the way of the apostles, through devout preaching, deeds of love, sacrifice, compassion, and confidence in the Holy Spirit. With extensive quotations from biblical, patristic, doctrinal, and canonical sources, this book is one of the most passionate and ardent defenses of the peaceful and nonmilitary missionary expansion of the Christian faith ever written.[57]

---

54. One apology is written in Spanish, published for the first time in 1958 (reproduced in *Obras completas*, Vol. 10, 101–93) and the other in Latin, published for the first time in 1975 (reproduced in *Obras completas*, Vol. 9, 43–667). Regarding the dispute between Las Casas and Sepúlveda, the standard text is Hanke, *All Mankind is One*.

55. Anthony Pagden, "Introduction," in *Las Casas on Columbus*, 9: ". . . until his death Las Casas remained convinced that the entire deleterious process of conquest could be undone if only those in authority would listen to his voice. All of his writings . . . were directed toward this end."

56. It was first printed in the twentieth century in a Latin and Spanish edition with a fine introduction by Lewis Hanke. Las Casas, *Del único modo de atraer a todos los pueblos a la verdadera religión*. It is reproduced in *Obras completas*, Vol. 2. There is an English version: Bartolomé de las Casas, *The Only Way*, edited by Helen Rand Parish and translated by Francis Patrick Sullivan.

57. It is hard to avoid the impression that Las Casas was under the influence of an author whose name he avoids for it had became disreputable in a nation under the shadow of the Inquisition: Erasmus of Rotterdam. There are resonances in his texts of the writings in which Erasmus censures Christianization by military force: *Dulce bellum*

It makes a powerful case for a peaceful non-military extension of the Christian faith as well as a strong critique of the linkage between cross and sword that, in Las Casas's view, was corrupting the evangelizing of the Native Americans. He considers the Spanish wars against the Native Americans illegal, immoral, and sinful. They violate human, natural, and divine law. It was, indeed, a theme of ardent discussion among Spaniard theologians for the entire sixteenth century.[58] Las Casas asks the Pope that his manuscript be examined by a board of theologians appointed by the Pope and its suggested policy be declared official doctrine of the church.[59]

inexpertis (1515), *Querela pacis* (1517), *Consultatio de bello turcico* (1530), and *Ecclesiastes sive concionator evangelicus* (1535). See Bataillon, *Erasme et l'Espagne*.

58. Vitoria deals will all possible pros and cons of the conquering first and converting afterwards approach in his *De Indis*, I. Sepúlveda was the most prestigious promoter of conversion *manu militari* in his book about the justice of the wars against the Native Americans. See his *Democrates secundus, sive de iustis belli causis*, in Sepúlveda, *Obras completas*, Vol. III, 38–134. Acosta, in his *De procuranda indorum salute*, defends the conjunction of military coercion and missionary persuasion, while, at the same time, trying to spell its limitations and mitigate its possible negative consequences. He argues that Las Casas's position does not take into account the ferocity and backwardness of the Native American "barbarians." See Rivera-Pagán, *La evangelización de los pueblos americanos*.

59. Is Las Casas a "pacifist"? In his letter to the Pope, he alludes to possible theoretical conditions required to render wars against infidels "just and legitimate." It is an awkward theme in the text, but it serves as a reminder that in several of his writings he distinguishes between unbelievers who have never attacked any Christian nation and those who have. The distinction basically refers to Native Americans and Muslims. Though there might be hypothetical reasons to justify war against the first, the history of their encounters shows, or so Las Casas thinks, that the Christians have always been the aggressors and oppressors and that, therefore, in their conflicts, the guilty ones are the Christians. On the contrary, in his view, the hostility between Christians and Muslims comes because the second have usurped lands of the first and are always attempting to subjugate the Christian nations.

Las Casas also accepts the traditional interpretation of Augustine's texts regarding state coercion of heretics, but rejects the attempts to expand that repressive norm to all infidels. He engages Sepúlveda in a discussion about Luke 14:23: "Compel people to come in . . ." (*compelle intrare*), a Gospel text cited by Augustine to justify state coercion of heretics. It was a much quoted biblical text in the theological debates regarding the conquering wars in Americas and it was also used to validate compulsory attendance of Native Americans to Christian proselytizing activities. See Rech, "Las Casas und die Kirchenväter," 26–43.

Las Casas differentiates between infidels who de iure and de facto are under the jurisdiction of Christian rulers (Jewish and Muslim minorities in Christian nations), those who are so de iure but not de facto (residents of lands formerly Christian but conquered by Muslim armies), and those who have never been so neither de iure nor de facto, like the Native Americans. And then there are the heretics, who are always de iure subject to

Why is it so urgent for the Church to condemn the military conquests of the Native American nations? Here comes a shocking statement, an eschatological warning to the Pope: ". . . so that the truth be not hidden for the damnation and destruction of the Church, as the time may come (which might be already at hand) in which God unveils our blemishes and our nakedness is shown to the whole pagan world." Las Casas had warned the Royal Council of Indies that the final Day of Judgment might be near and that it may entail the eternal damnation of Spain. Now he admonishes the Pope that unless the Church acts decisively on behalf of the oppressed Native Americans, it might also find itself condemned in that imminent fateful Doomsday. That day, he suggests, the Church might appear as blemished and naked in comparison with the Gentiles and infidels. For a bishop to admonish a Pope in this manner is, indeed, a dramatic act of audacity.

But this is just the prologue to other daring requests to the Pope. Veiled as petitions, they are rather radical challenges to the Church. Las Casas demands from the Pope an official normative declaration regarding the affairs of the Indies with its corresponding anathemas.

> Since so many are the flatterers who in secret, like dogs with rabies, bark against the truth, to Your Beatitude I humbly beseech that a decree be enacted in which are declared excommunicated and anathema, all those who affirm that wars against the infidels are just if waged to combat idolatry, or for the convenience of spreading the Gospel, specially in regard to those infidels who have never injured or are not injuring us.

Idolatry was frequently used as a *casus belli* against the Native Americans. Columbus invoked idolatry as a justification to begin the American slave trade.[60] Hernán Cortés initiated the war against Tenochtitlán only after formally declaring it a crusade against idolatry.[61] Sepúlveda, among

---

the Catholic Church and state. The possible legitimacy of military force or state coercion against unbelievers differs, therefore, according to their specific category of infidelity. Thus, the same state that might be justified in waging war against the Ottomans and strengthening the Inquisition against the heretics, should refrain from military actions against the Native Americans.

Las Casas, however, leans towards a negative appraisal of war, for "war . . . is the most wretched and pestilential of all things under heaven and is utterly opposed to Christ's life and teaching" (*In Defense of the Indians*, 359).

60. Columbus, *New and Fresh English Translation of the Letter of Columbus Announcing the Discovery of America*, 14: "Their Highnesses can see that I shall give them . . . slaves, as many as they shall order, who will be idolaters."

61. Hernán Cortés, *Documentos cortesianos*, 165: "In as much . . . the natives of these

A Prophetic Challenge to the Church

others, had emphasized idolatry as a legitimate reason to conquer the Native Americans through war, for idolatry is not only a grave blasphemy against divine and natural law in itself, but also the source of their alleged moral depravements: human sacrifice, cannibalism, and sodomy. The Franciscan missionaries rationalized Cortés's conquest as a divine punishment against the idolatry of the natives, and tried to explain to the Mexican elders the demonic origin of their religious practices.[62] The condemnation of sacrilegious idolatry became a benchmark for the conquest and enslaving of native communities.[63] The "extirpation of idolatry," so well studied regarding Perú by Pierre Duviols, was one of the ideological foundations of what Robert Ricard aptly named the spiritual conquest of the autochthonous communities.[64] Therefore, Las Casas's request to the Pope that the invocation of idolatry for doing violence to the Native Americans be declared anathema goes to the heart of one of the main ideological resources behind the conquest of the Americas. The demand is grandiose, as will also be the silence of Rome.

The second principle that Las Casas requests to be included in the Papal decree of anathemas is one very dear to his mind.

> Or those who assert that the infidels are not true lords and owners of their properties; or those who affirm that they are unable to understand and receive the Gospel and eternal salvation, on the basis of their alleged lack of intelligence or acuity of mind, which in fact they do not lack, those Indians whose rights I have defended till my death, for the honor of God and the Church.

---

regions have a culture and veneration of idols, which is a great disservice to God Our Lord, and the devil blinds and deceives them . . . I propose to bring them to the knowledge of our Holy Catholic faith . . . Let us go to uproot the natives of these regions from those idolatries . . . so that they will come to the knowledge of God and of His Holy Catholic faith."

62. Duverger, *La Conversion des Indiens de Nouvelle-Espagne*.

63. Vitoria, Las Casas, and Acosta, however, pace Sepúlveda, perceive the difficulty of using the Old Testament injunctions against idolatry as models for the Christianization of the Native Americans. What is at stake in the Old Testament is the extirpation of idolatry by means of the extermination of the idolaters. The Spanish enterprise, however, is missionary. It attempts to extirpate idolatry by means of the conversion of the idolaters, not their annihilation. In many parts of the Americas, however, the end result was similar: the elimination of idolatry thanks to the death of the idolaters.

64. Duviols, *La lutte contre les religions autochtones dans le Pérou colonial*; Ricard, *Spiritual Conquest of Mexico*.

Are the Native Americans equal to the Europeans in rationality and free will? This was, alas, a crucial question during the Christian expansion in early modernity. Aristotle's vision of the distinction between the Greeks, as a people of culture, and the "barbarians," and his discussion of just war and slavery in the first part of his *Politics*, were refurbished in the encounter between Christian Europeans and the indigenous American communities.[65] His arguments regarding the justice of warfare against the barbarians and their legitimate enslavement became relevant for the sixteenth-century theological discussions on war and slavery.[66] "Barbarian" became a frequent term of reference to the Native Americans. It is found in Francisco de Vitoria,[67] Sepúlveda,[68] and in many other sixteenth-century writers. Probably the best definition of what was meant by "barbarian" is provided by José de Acosta: "We call 'Indians' all the Barbarians that have been discovered in our time by the Spanish and the Portuguese . . . people who are not only deprived of the light of the Gospel but also unaware of civilization."[69] Barbarians are ignorant of both Christian faith and literary culture. They lack knowledge of Christ and of the alphabet.[70] They are, therefore, inferior.[71] Thus, according to the discourse of several court intellectuals, like

---

65. *Politics*, book I. Bruno Rech analyses the way Las Casas read Aristotle in his article "Bartolomé de las Casas und Aristoteles," 39–68.

66. Hanke, *Aristotle and the American Indians*; Anthony Pagden, *Fall of Natural Man*.

67. *De Indis*, I, 233: "This whole dispute . . . has arisen again because of these barbarians in the New World, commonly called Indians, who came under the power of the Spaniards some forty years ago . . ." Nestor Capdevila points out a crucial semantic difference between Vitoria and Las Casas. While the first refers to the Native Americans as *barbaros . . . quos indos vulgo vocant* ("barbarians commonly called Indians"), Las Casas alludes to them as *Novi Orbi habitatores, quos vulgo Indos appelamus* ("inhabitants of the New World, which we commonly call Indians"). Capdevila (*Las Casas: une politique de l'humanité*, 270). For the literary context of the two quotations, see *Obras de Francisco de Vitoria*, 642 and Las Casas, *Obras completas*, Vol. 9, 76.

68. *Democrates secundus*, 39: "If the war with which the monarchs of Spain have subjugated and attempt to subjugate under their dominion those barbarians . . . commonly called Indians . . . is just or not . . . is a very important issue."

69. *De procuranda indorum salute*, 4.

70. Regarding the ontological distinction between literary and oral peoples, see Mignolo, *The Darker Side of the Renaissance*.

71. See Rivera-Pagán, "Qui est l'Indien? Humanité ou bestialité de l'indigène américain," 33–51. Acosta oscillates between attributing to them bestiality or childish immaturity. In an earlier draft of his *Democrates secundus*, Sepúlveda tended to ape them, and Vasco de Quiroga bishop of Michoacán, considers them as children in need of paternal guidance. Quiroga, *Información en derecho* (1535).

A Prophetic Challenge to the Church

Sepúlveda, the Native Americans are unfit for self-government. They can be considered *natura servi*, fated by nature to servitude.[72] For their own benefit, civilized Christians should rule them. If they resist, the war to subjugate them is, in principle, just and legitimate.

Las Casas devoted an extended section of his Apology against Sepúlveda to refute the vilification of the Native Americans implied by their categorization as barbarians.[73] He also penned an ambitious and long manuscript on their cultural and cultic traditions, to prove the dignity of their culture and religiosity. That text—*Apologética historia sumaria*—is the longer and most passionate defense of the Native American cultures written in the sixteenth century.[74] It also inaugurated a romantic tradition, which through Montaigne forged the mythical image of the *bon sauvage*.[75]

In the letter to the Pope, Las Casas comes back to this crucial issue and requests a decree of anathema against any denial or degradation of the rationality of the Native Americans, their personal liberty,[76] their right for public sovereignty or private ownership, or their ability to understand and accept the mysteries of the Christian faith. In all those essential dimensions of humanness, insists Las Casas, there is no fundamental ontological distinction between Europeans and Native Americans, and thus no legitimate justification for dispossessing them of their political sovereignty, their private goods, their personal freedom, or for abrogating their right to the

---

72. *Democrates secundus*, 130. On the debate about whether the Native Americans were slaves by nature and the ways Aristotle was read in that discussion, see Celestino del Arenal, "La teoría de la servidumbre natural," 67–124.

73. In this context, it might be appropriate to recall Montaigne's famous dictum in his essay "Des cannibales" (1580): "chacun appelle barbarie ce qui n'est pas de son usage." *Essais*, Vol. I, 344.

74. *Apologética historia sumaria*. As many of Las Casas's writings, it was first published in its integrity only in the twentieth century (1909). *Obras completas*, Vols. 6–8.

75. Luzio, "Bartolomé de las Casas y Michel de Montaigne," 223–85; Abellán, "Los orígenes españoles del mito del 'buen salvaje,'" 157–79; and Maravall, "Utopía y primitivismo en Las Casas," 311–88. Maravall's description of Las Casas as a "Rousseau *avant la lettre*" (ibid., 350) and Bruno Rech's assertion that the Spanish bishop is a "Vorläufer von Rousseau" ("Las Casas und die Kirchenväter," 35) are misleading. The sixteenth-century theologian and the eighteenth-century philosopher are both counter-cultural and were both viewed in their times as *enfant terribles*, but they inhabit very different theoretical and ideological niches, as Nestor Capdevila (*Las Casas: une politique de l'humanité*, 66–76) and Gustavo Gutiérrez (*Las Casas*, 299–301) have emphasized.

76. Whether it was legitimate to enslave Native Americans was a controversial issue among sixteenth-theologians and jurists. See Rivera-Pagán, "Freedom and Servitude: Indigenous Slavery in the Spanish Conquest of the Caribbean," 316–62.

ecclesiastical sacraments.⁷⁷ A much quoted text of the *Apologética* gives expression to the principle that underlies his lifelong exertions: "All the nations of the world are human and all share in the same definition: they are rational beings. All have intellect and will, as created in God's image and similitude."⁷⁸

This has been the core of his struggles of more than five decades, for the sake of, as he writes to the Pope, "those Indians whose rights I have defended till my death, for the honor of God and the Church." Now, at the moment in which death is the only future for his flesh, he recapitulates that long dispute, in a sharp request to the *Vicarius Christi* to rebuke and condemn all those who question or deny the rationality, the political rights, the personal liberty of the Native Americans,⁷⁹ or their capability to understand and profess the Christian faith. And then, always certain of his ability to persuade by means of logical argumentations and authoritative references, Las Casas concludes: "In my book I have clearly shown that all those assertions are against the sacred canons, as well as against natural law and the commandments of the Gospel, and I will confirm it even more, if

---

77. The Spanish theologians and missionaries debated the capability of the Native Americans to participate in the sacraments. Acosta defends their right to six of the seven sacraments but opposes their priestly ordination, for it is wrong to consecrate to the ministry "the dregs of the people." *De procuranda indorum salute*, Vol. II, 146.

78. *Apologética historia sumaria*, c. 48; *Obras completas*, Vol. 7, 536.

79. Las Casas's view of the slavery of another people, the Africans forcefully imported to the New World, is the object of a long bibliography. Among the most important contributions are: Zavala, "¿Las Casas esclavista?," 149–54; Brady, "Role of Las Casas in the Emergence of Negro Slavery in the New World," 43–55; Ortiz, "La leyenda negra contra fray Bartolomé de las Casas," 146–84 and 84–116; Pérez Fernández, en Las Casas, *Brevísima relación de la destrucción de Africa*; and Dussel, *Política de la liberación*, 233. Despite the attempts of several of these scholars to present Las Casas as a strong defender of the liberty and political rights of both, Native Americans and Africans, in his last texts, like the letter to the Council of Indies and the Pope, the issue of black slavery is absent, at a time in which, however, the African slave trade was increasing exponentially. I have tried to develop a more nuanced view of Las Casas's complex perspective on this issue in "Bartolomé de las Casas y la esclavitud africana," 83–110. See also Wilson, "Black slaves and messianic dreams" and Capdevila, *Las Casas: une politique de l'humanité*, 79–87. For the general issue involved, see Davis, *Problem of Slavery in Western Culture* and Quenum, *Les Églises chrétiennes et la traite atlantique du XVe au XIXe siècle*. From a rather apologetic perspective, the Papal decrees regarding the beginnings of the African slave trade by Christian Europeans are minutiously analysed by Charles-Martial de Witte, "Les bulles pontificales et l'expansion portugaise au XVe siècle," in several issues of *Revue d'histoire ecclésiastique*.

that were possible, for I have exhaustively researched and corroborated this matter."

The next three requests to the Pope have to do with the identity, vocation, and mission of the Christian Church in the New World. Mindful of the way in which the Royal Patronage has modeled a Church loyal to the State, Las Casas admonishes the Roman Pontiff that he should

> Order the bishops of the Indies that, under holy obedience, they be concerned about those natives, who, with hard labors and tyrannies (more than what it could be believed), carry on their meager shoulders, against all natural and divine law, a heavy yoke and unbearable load, which makes it necessary that Your Holiness instruct those bishops to defend their cause, becoming a protecting wall for them, even to spill their own blood, as by divine law they are obliged, and that in no way they accept their appointment, if the King and his Council would not support them and uproot so many tyrannies and oppressions.

The Church as the protector and defender of the Native Americans: that, in short, is his audacious request to the Pontiff, the vision of this obstinate and pugnacious dying bishop and prophet. Such conduct, according to Las Casas, is not optional. It is not a model of behavior that the Church might or might not assume. The bishops are obliged to follow this daring and perilous conduct "by natural and divine law," even if it entails the way of the cross, the sufferings and death of martyrdom.[80] Instead of the bishops pledging their fealty to the state policies, as done by the first American bishops in the Burgos capitulations, they should demand from the court an oath of support in the uprooting of "so many tyrannies and oppressions," before accepting their nominations to their dioceses.

Las Casas probably has in mind his previous failed attempt to use the power of the episcopacy in Chiapas to make right a situation of social oppression. If, he seems to be suggesting, this time the Pope intervenes with a clear mandate to the American bishops and is willing to steer the Church

---

80. Antonio de Valdivieso, bishop of Nicaragua, was assassinated in 1550 by a group of Spaniards irritated by his censure of their mistreatment of the natives. Gonzalez Dávila, *Teatro eclesiástico de la primitiva iglesia de la Nueva España en las Indias Occidentales* (1649), Vol. II, 157–59. Enrique Dussel has written on sixteenth-century bishops as "protectors of the Indians." Dussel, *Les évêques hispano-américains: défenseurs et évangélisateurs de l'indien (1504–1620)*. On the assassination of another Central American bishop, 430 years later, see Rivera-Pagán, "For Times Such As This. Oscar Romero: Bishop, Prophet, Martyr," 89–107.

in the direction of becoming the defender and protector of the indigenous communities, then there is hope for the future. Therein lies his audacious request to the Roman Pontiff.

The next petition has to do with a sensitive issue in the evangelization of the Native Americans during the sixteenth century: language. Las Casas indicates the problem with his usual judgmental tone, but also with uncommon brevity: "Openly and unjustly the bishop ignores the language of his subjects, and does not attempt to learn it well." Therefore, the Pope should order that the American prelates learn the native languages. "I humbly beseech Your Beatitude to order them to master the language of their sheep, showing that they are so commanded by divine and natural law, for at the moment many awful indignities occur . . . caused by the negligence of the bishops in learning the language of their parishioners."

One of the most impressive achievements of the contemporary Spanish missionary efforts had to do precisely with the alphabetization of the Native languages and the translation of homilies, liturgies, religious plays, prayers, and biblical texts, into them. Yet, as Acosta would note two decades later, this was mainly the labor of friars within the religious orders. Most diocesan bishops and priests were reluctant to invest the time and energy required by the mastery of those languages. The debate whether to encourage the priesthood to learn the native languages or, on the contrary, to compel the natives to learn Spanish, frequently pitted the religious orders against the regular ecclesiastical ministry. This linguistic dilemma has to do with the proper communication of the Christian faith. But, as Las Casas is convinced, at a deeper level, it has also to do with the quality and character of its inculturation. Inculturation of the faith, in analogy to the Incarnation, begins with linguistic assimilation as an immersion in the culture of a community and its particular symbolic universe.[81] The identification of the Church with the indigenous cultures has to traverse inevitably the complex path of linguistic identity.

If the previous requests are difficult to satisfy, the last one is even harder. The Church has not only to defend the Native Americans and to assimilate their language and culture; it should also share their poverty, their dispossession. The American Church, however, is getting immensely rich in material goods thanks to the exploitation of the land and the work of the

---

81. Linguistic translation and inculturation, as analogical implications of the doctrine of the incarnation, have become important themes in modern missiological theology. See Sanneh, *Translating the Message* and Walls, *Missionary Movement in Christian History*.

A Prophetic Challenge to the Church

Native Americans. Several years later Acosta will bewail the enrichment of priests and bishops, but will consider it a minor price in exchange for the preaching of the Christian faith.[82] Not Las Casas. For the Bishop of Chiapas it constitutes a sinful scandal. "Immense scandal and no less detriment to our most holy religion is that in such a new place bishops and friars and priests are getting rich and live sumptuously, while their recently converted subjects remain in so great and incredible poverty, that many of them die daily in profound misery, due to the tyranny, hunger and excessive work that they suffer."

The contrast between ecclesiastical enrichment and the poverty of the Native Americans entails, for Las Casas, an intensely severe sentence: the Church is guilty of complicity in the dispossession, misery, and desolation of the autochthonous communities. Herein lies the acuteness of his initial admonition that in the Day of Judgment the Church might be revealed to the Gentile nations as naked and blemished. The Church cannot reproach the conquistadores or encomenderos if she does not deal with her own complicity in the social and economic oppression of the indigenous peoples. Thus, the drastic and radical challenge of the dying bishop to the Pope.

> Therefore, to Your Holiness I humbly beseech to declare those ministers to be obliged by natural and divine law, as in fact they are, to restitute all the gold, silver, and precious stones they have acquired, for their wealth is taken from human beings who endure extreme need and who today live in misery, with whom, by divine and natural law, they are even beholden to share their own possessions.

From his 1514 homily, when for the first time he denounced the enslavement of the Native Americans, till this last text, fifty-two years later, one theme is constantly repeated in the writings of Las Casas: the salvation of the Christians depends upon their disposition to restitute everything they have acquired by conquest and slavery. The duty of restitution is at the heart of the sacrament of penance and at the core of Las Casas's episcopal practice, prophetic message, and theological disquisition.[83] The surprising conclusion, therefore, of Las Casas's letter to the Pope, is that in the history-

---

82. *De procuranda indorum salute*, Vol. I, 143: "For that is what the Spaniards are looking for after such a long ocean voyage, and it is through the metals [gold and silver] that commerce works, that the judges preside, and more often than not the priests preach the Gospel."

83. Cantú, "Evoluzione e significato della dottrina della restituzione in Bartolomé de las Casas," 55–143, 231–19.

making encounter between Christian Europeans and Native American infidels, what is mainly at stake and in doubt is the salvation of the first, the Christian Europeans. They—the Spanish state and the Roman Church—are called to do penance and to beg for divine forgiveness and absolution. This is indeed an extraordinary inversion of the usual understanding of the matter, in the history of the global expansion of the Christian faith.

Only then, after dispatching his farewell letters to the Royal Council of Indies and to the Pope,[84] could this bold and old bishop, theologian, and prophet rest in peace, eternally.[85] Only then, could Las Casas, as the biblical Simeon (Luke 2:29), exclaim: *Nunc dimittis servuum tuum, Domine . . . in pace.*

APPENDIX

Bartolomé de las Casas's *Petition to His Holiness Pope Pius V* (1566) (my translation)

What things are necessary for the correct way of preaching the Gospel to the infidels, and to render just and legitimate the wars against them, I have declared in the book that I sent to Your Beatitude, and I hope to expand them further. To Your Beatitude I beseech intensively, by the blood of our Redemption, to command that my book be examined and, if found right, that it be stamped, so that the truth be not hidden for the damnation and destruction of the Church, as the time may come (which might be already at hand) in which God unveils our blemishes and our nakedness is shown to the whole pagan world.

Since so many are the flatterers who in secret, like dogs with rabies, bark against the truth, to Your Beatitude I humbly beseech that a decree be enacted in which are declared excommunicated and anathema, all those

---

84. Luciano Pereña, Isacio Pérez Fernández, and Marianne Mahn-Lot argue that certain instructions of Pope Pius V regarding the Native Americans were probably influenced by Las Casas's letter and were the Papal response to it. Pereña, "Estudio preliminar," a Bartolomé de las Casas, *De regia potestate*, cxii–cxiii; Pérez Fernández, *Inventario documentado de los escritos*, 773–76; and Mahn-Lot, *Bartolomé de las Casas et le droit des indiens*, 247, 260. I do not find their arguments compelling and certainly those Papal instructions fell considerably short from the bold demands of Las Casas.

85. It falls beyond the scope of this essay to examine the ways in which Latin American liberation theologians have read Las Casas. It might be symptomatic that the longest and, in my opinion, most enticing book up to now written by Gustavo Gutiérrez is his monograph on Las Casas.

who affirm that wars against the infidels are just if waged to combat idolatry, or for the convenience of spreading the Gospel, specially in regard to those infidels who have never injured or are not injuring us. Or those who assert that the infidels are not true lords and owners of their properties; or those who affirm that they are unable to understand and receive the Gospel and eternal salvation, on the basis of their alleged lack of intelligence or acuity of mind, which in fact they do not lack, those Indians whose rights I have defended till my death, for the honor of God and the Church. In my book I have clearly shown that all those assertions are against the sacred canons, as well as against natural law and the commandments of the Gospel, and I will confirm it even more, if that were possible, for I have exhaustively researched and corroborated this matter.

As experience, teacher of all things, confirms that in these times it is necessary to renew all the canons that command the bishops to take care of the captives, of afflicted men and widows, even to the point in which their blood might be shed for them, as they are obliged by natural and divine law, to Your Beatitude I humbly beseech that, by the renewal of those canons, order the bishops of the Indies that, under holy obedience, they be concerned about those natives, who, with hard labors and tyrannies (more than what it could be believed), carry on their meager shoulders, against all natural and divine law, a heavy yoke and unbearable load, which makes it necessary that Your Holiness instruct those bishops to defend their cause, becoming a protecting wall for them, even to spill their own blood, as by divine law they are obliged, and that in no way they accept their appointment, if the King and his Council would not support them and uproot so many tyrannies and oppressions.

Openly and unjustly the bishop ignores the language of his subjects, and does not attempt to learn it well. Therefore, I humbly beseech Your Beatitude to order them to master the language of their sheep, showing that they are so commanded by divine and natural law, for at the moment many awful indignities occur in the presence of Your Holiness, caused by the negligence of the bishops in learning the language of their parishioners.

Immense scandal and no less detriment to our most holy religion is that in such a new place bishops and friars and priests are getting rich and live sumptuously, while their recently converted subjects remain in so great and incredible poverty, that many of them die daily in profound misery, due to the tyranny, hunger and excessive work that they suffer. Therefore, to Your Holiness I humbly beseech to declare those ministers to be obliged by natural and divine law, as in fact they are, to restitute all the gold, silver, and precious stones they have acquired, for their wealth is taken from human beings who endure extreme need and who today live in misery, with whom, by divine and natural law, they are even beholden to share their own possessions.

2

A View from Below
Female Lament and Defiance in Times of War[1]

Woe, woe is me!
What words, or cries, or lamentations can I utter?
Ah me! for the sorrows of my closing years!
for slavery too cruel to brook or bear! . . .
Where is any god or power divine to succour me? . . .
Life on earth has no more charm for me . . .
Queen of sorrows.

—EURIPIDES[2]

To the women of Afghanistan and Iraq, that we may hear the lamentations of their hearts . . .

The image does not vanish from either my mind or my heart. A house destroyed in Iraq by coalition forces battling resistance insurgents. "Collateral damage" is the sanitized and cynical term coined for this kind of tragic mistake. A family decimated, some members killed, others wounded, the

---

1. Paper read in "'The View From Below,' The Bonhoeffer Lectures on Public Ethics." October 12, 2004. Wesley Theological Seminary, Washington, DC.

2. Euripides, *Hecuba*, 26.

survivors walking in shock, as lifeless specters. An old Iraqi woman, the matriarch of the family, stands in the middle of what used to be her house, and raises her gaunt face and wrinkled hands to the sky. Her countenance is an expression of immense affliction. Is she praying, crying to her God, cursing, or just wailing her profound distress? Is it an act of lamentation, of defiance, or both? We do not know and will probably never know.

Her photographic depiction, alas, will never fade away from my memory. It has become another portrait of the sorrows and pains inflicted by war upon the souls and bodies of women.[3] The image of that suffering, praying, cursing, lamenting, defiant Iraqi woman is the Ariadne's thread of this essay, its guiding leitmotiv even through what for some readers might be its labyrinthine incursions into classical Hellenic literature. It belongs to the tradition of Francisco Goya's powerful and horrifying etchings *The Disasters of War*.

SIMONE WEIL AND THE TRAGIC EPIC OF WAR

"The true hero, the real subject, the core of the *Iliad*, is might."[4] Thus begins Simone Weil's "The *Iliad*, Poem of Might," her splendid meditation on the most eminent Hellenic poetic text. It is a magnificent *tour de force*. The delicate and sensitive Weil, a prematurely withered genius, contemplates the sorrows and horrors of war, the cruelties and violence committed in the name of so many proclaimed ideals, in the altar of so many deceptively sacralized words. Weil pays tribute in a beautiful way to the awful immensity of the griefs and pains, the dashed hopes and illusions, caused by the violence of war.

Yet, also evident is the immense admiration that Weil feels reading the *Iliad*. She relishes in the aesthetic grace of Homeric Greek (the learned Weil read the *Iliad* in its original language): "nothing of all that the peoples of Europe have produced is worth the first poem to have appeared among them."[5] And, most of all, she deeply admires the courage of Patroclus, Hector, or Achilles when their turn to confront fate and death comes. There can be no doubt about the preference of this woman, of Jewish ancestry, for

---

3. On the portraits of the violence and sorrows of war, see Sontag, *Regarding the Pain of Others*.

4. Weil, "*Iliad*, Poem of Might," 153. The original reads: "Le vrai héros, le vrai sujet, le centre de l'*Iliade*, c'est la force." Weil, "L'*Iliade* ou le poème de la force," tome 2:3, 227.

5. "*Iliad*, Poem of Might," 183.

Homer over Moses, for the *Iliad* over *Genesis*, for the Greek language and culture over the Hebrew language and culture (also over the Roman culture and language).

Affliction is the unavoidable consequence of all human wars, cursed by the caprice and malice of the gods and by the human proclivity towards violence and force.[6] The human soul is overwhelmed by the rage and affliction of Achilles, saddened by the death of his dearest friend, Patroclus, impressed by the courage of Hector, beaten and mercilessly killed by Achilles, and, according to Weil, awed also by the agony of Jesus, when the hour of his arrest, torment, and execution is near.[7] "Unless protected by an armour of lies, man cannot endure might without suffering a blow in the depth of his soul."[8] Not many writers would join in the same story Achilles and Jesus!

War, according to Weil's elegant essay, is always very near, too near indeed, to the human heart. No other human endeavor compares to war in its ability to achieve the terrifying process of converting a human being into a *thing*, a non-person. By transforming living bodies into corpses, spiritual life into mere matter, and by inspiring overwhelming cruelty and violence in hearts where, on many previous occasions, tenderness and mercy have reigned, war becomes the most dehumanizing of all human enterprises. It spreads affliction and agony across all social and intimate borders. It poisons the human heart and dissolves compassion. In the reign of violence, of the immense destruction and affliction unleashed by human bellicosity, "there is no room for either justice or prudence."[9]

The transformation of victim and victimizer from human beings into things is painfully shown in Achilles' refusal to heed the supplications of Hector and Priam. Hector has killed Patroclus and must therefore die in the hands of Achilles. No tears of a father, a wife or a son, will protect the brave Trojan prince from his fateful destiny.[10] And Achilles knows very well that he also, the killer of Hector, must die young, victim of a violent rage similar

---

6. See her essay, "Love of God and Affliction," 439–68.

7. "*Iliad*, Poem of Might," 180: "The accounts of the Passion show that a divine spirit united to the flesh is altered by affliction, trembles before suffering and death, feels himself, at the moment of deepest agony, separated from men and from God."

8. Ibid., 182.

9. Ibid., 163.

10. Weil's translation and reading of Achilles' rejection of Priam's supplication has been disputed. See Benfey, "Tale of Two Iliads," 82. Yet Benfey's critique does not affect the core of Weil's argument, namely, that the raging violence of war impedes Achilles from heeding the supplication of a father, Priam, anguished by the fate of his son, Hector.

to his, away from the loving care of mother or lover. Affliction, courage, destruction, and death: these are the consequences of war. And the choice of war, that most lethal of all human enterprises, seems to elude personal liberty and ethical deliberation. War seems to be an unavoidable dimension of human destiny, so fated and cursed by the gods. *Thanatos* triumphs over *eros* or *agape*, this seems a reasonable way of reading the *Iliad*.

The *Iliad* is therefore, according to Weil, more than a magnificent and beautiful epic poem. It also discloses the tragic mystery of human violence, the ways in which human beings ceaselessly mutate into instruments of death and devastation. Fate and tragedy rule tyrannically over human affairs. Good and evil human beings are both crushed by the same violence that periodically demonically possesses human history. The discovery of this fateful truth is the great achievement of classic Greece, poetically narrated first by Homer's epic, then by Attic tragedy, and finally by the Gospels—"the last and most marvelous expression of Greek genius, as the *Iliad* is its first expression."[11]

Weil's essay is doubtless an expression of her love for the classic Greek culture,[12] but it is more than that. It is also a deeply sensitive, eloquent, and serene meditation on the manners in which war destroys human culture and, even more importantly, human compassion. It was published in December 1940 and January 1941, in the French journal *Cahiers du Sud*, at a crucial moment when Europe was beginning its engulfment in the vortex of the most savage war that history has ever experienced. It is both a warning against any kind of romantic beautification of war, by means of the ideological manipulations of solemn words—fatherland, race, nation, God, religion, liberty—and a convocation to epic and stoic confrontation of the merciless fate, death, and destruction entailed by war.

Her essay is a warning and evocation she knows very well will not be heeded. For, according to Weil, the modern state is a Leviathan poised to oppress and devour by means of the constant mobilization and preparation for war. Thus it achieves its goal of "the total effacement of the individual before the state bureaucracy."[13] If Weil admires the dignified and courageous ethos of the tragic Homeric heroes, she has nothing but contempt for modern technological warfare and for the states that wage it (whatever

---

11. "*Iliad*, Poem of Might," 180.

12. Weil's writings display her love for the Hellenic culture as well as her peculiar disdain for the Hebrew and Roman roots of Western civilization.

13. "Reflection's on War," 246.

their ideological pigmentations). It is a "most atrocious" activity, "the most radical form of oppression," for soldiers, in modern warfare, "do not expose themselves to death, they are sent to slaughter." It transforms the relationship between state and citizens into "despotism and enslavement" and "calculated murder."[14]

No epic poem like the *Iliad* could be composed in honor of the modern system of devastation. For "modern war is absolutely different from everything designated by that name under earlier regimes."[15] It creates immense miseries devoid of any human integrity. There are no more tragic heroic warriors, like Agamemnon, Hector, Patroclus, or Achilles, but expendable pawns trained to slaughter and be slaughtered. No supplications are refused, for no supplications are heard. Painful lamentations are uttered, but they are immediately drowned by the cascade of chauvinistic propaganda, with its loquacious public convincers, and by the cynical conversion of military destruction into electronic spectacle.

This radical rejection of modern technological warfare leads Weil into an agonizing dilemma: What to do regarding the fascist and Nazi menace? Before the German invasion first of Poland and then of France, Weil assumed a firm position against war, for "weapons yielded by a sovereign state apparatus can bring no one liberty."[16] In case war erupts, she counsels revolt against the military machine of one's own state.

It is a desperate and forlorn situation, she knows it well. "But the helplessness one feels . . . cannot exempt one from remaining faithful to oneself." Thus, she proclaims resistance not against the possible invading enemy, but against the state and military apparatus "that calls itself our defender and makes us slaves."[17] She will discover the fragility of that position when the Nazi and fascist armies begin to spread devastation all over Europe, as never before since the Thirty Years War (1618–1648). Then the immense lamentations uttered by so many distressed and downtrodden human beings will provoke a deep sorrow in Weil's sensitive soul that will escort her into the shadows of her own death. Death was sometimes the ultimate consolation for a delicate spirit unable to cope with the tensions of an epoch so aptly called the "Age of Extremes."[18] As befits a lover of the *Iliad*

14. Ibid., 242, 246.
15. Ibid., 241.
16. Ibid., 242.
17. Ibid., 248.
18. Hobsbawm, *Age of Extremes*.

and the Greek tragedies, she faced death with the fortitude of an epic heroine. Fortunately, she also left us an amazing literary heritage[19] that might provide a perspective to meditate upon our own times, an age when ...

> Things fall apart; the centre cannot hold
> The blood-dimmed tide is loosed, and everywhere
> The ceremony of innocence is drowned ...[20]

EURIPIDES AND THE WOES OF THE TROJAN WOMEN

When revisited in the context of today's theoretical debates, one is struck by the glaring absence in Weil's "The *Iliad*, Poem of Might" of a feminist gaze. The essay deals splendidly with the tragic and dignified manner in which Patroclus, Achilles, Hector, Agamemnon, and Priam confront fate and death, to be finally crushed by the violence unleashed by war. A man, a male hero, stands in the center of her meditation on the *Iliad*, as well as in her allusions to the Attic tragedies of Aeschylus and Sophocles, and to the Jesus of the Gospels. One could even perceive a certain seduction in Weil's contemplation of the Homeric heroes, a paradoxical fascination of the courageous dignity with which these warriors assume their tragic destiny and curse. But, what about the Trojan women? Curiously, this very sensitive and perceptive woman and writer, Simone Weil, silences them. A writer that would never heed Aristotle's apothegm—"Woman, silence is the grace of woman"[21]—ends up by silencing the female victims of the *Iliad*'s courageous heroes.[22]

Weil clearly understands the awful consequences of the destruction of a city, be it Troy, Warsaw, or Paris. And yet, as she follows the *Iliad*'s concern with Patroclus, Achilles, Hector, Agamemnon, and Priam, something important is missed: the agonies and sorrows of Iphigenia, Hecuba, Andromache, Cassandra, Polyxena, and Helen, the female protagonists of the Trojan conflict. It is an epic poem of war and force, therefore, Weil seems to be saying, men, not women, should always take the center stage. She seems to overlook that the city is also the place where women not only give birth to human existence, but also confer meaning and coherence to

19. Coles, *Simone Weil: A Modern Pilgrimage*.
20. Yeats, "Second Coming," 820.
21. Aristotle, *Politics*, Bk. I, 1260a 30. Aristotle is quoting Sophocles, "Ajax," 293.
22. For a different perspective, see Courtine-Denamy, *Three Women in Dark Times: Edith Stein, Hannah Arendt, Simone Weil*.

the life they have procreated. The destruction of a city entails therefore not only the death of the warriors, but also the enduring misery and distress of captive women. Thus the anonymous author of the biblical *Lamentations* poignantly feminizes the devastated city of Jerusalem:

> How lonely sits the city
> that once was full of people!
> How like a widow she has become,
> she that was great among the nations!
>
> She that was a princess among the provinces
> has become a vassal.
>
> She weeps bitterly in the night,
> with tears on her cheeks;
> among all her lovers she has no one to comfort her;
> all her friends have dealt treacherously with her,
> they have become her enemies.[23]

The curse of war, violence and blood as unavoidable human destiny, seems to be the tragic enigma so beautifully displayed in the earliest Hellenic epic poem. Weil indicates the diverse instances in which that iron law of human destruction could have been disavowed. If only Agamemnon, Achilles, Odysseus, or Hector would have been more moderate in their words or actions . . . And yet, the warriors seem unable to free themselves from the bloody fascination with Ares, the merciless god of war. The curse of war proceeds unimpeded on its path of death and devastation. Yes, indeed, but what about the affliction suffered by the mothers, wives, daughters, lovers, or sisters of the heroic warriors? What about the agonizing sorrow felt by the female nourishers of human existence when struck by the pathos of ferocious destruction? What about the misery visited upon those women who have never wielded a sword or spear and have never curtailed prematurely the life of another fellow human being?

Weil shares the preference of many of her contemporaries for the "classic" style of Aeschylus' and Sophocles' tragedies over Euripides's more secular and profane outlook. Yet, it was Euripides who never forgot that the Trojan War began not only with the abduction of Helen, a matter to which he devoted one play, but also with the sacrifice of Iphigenia, the unfortunate

---

23. *Lamentations* 1:1–2. With the exception of *Job*, Weil tends to disregard with contempt the Hebrew sacred scriptures.

young daughter of Agamemnon and Clytemnestra.[24] The wars of men seem to require, at their beginning or at their conclusions, the sacrifice of a young maiden, be it that of Iphigenia, so that the war against Troy may proceed; that of Polyxena, the young daughter of Priam and Hecuba, sacrificed by Neoptolemus at Achilles' tomb, so that the ships of the victorious Greeks may depart for home;[25] or that of the nameless daughter of Jephthah, so that the vow between her father, the male commander of the Hebrew forces, and Yahweh, the Lord of Hosts, may be fulfilled.[26] These stories seem to question Freud's thesis that the source of human religiosity is the sacrifice, by the band of sons and brothers, of the mythical primeval father,[27] and suggest that one should rather look into the sacrifice of a virginal daughter of the Patriarch as the matrix of ritual practices of expiation and atonement. Men make war; the gods lust for the blood and flesh of young virgins.

It is also Euripides who in one of his more popular tragedies gives careful attention to the female lamentations in the midst of the Trojan War. He knows well that after the noisy devastation of war ceases, another clamor resounds, "the endless cries of captured women, assigned as slaves to various Greeks."[28] In *The Women of Troy*, the plight of Hecuba, Andromache, and Cassandra is voiced. Not the brave and epic heroism of men of war, but the sorrows of the women who suffer its sinister consequences constitute the focus of this splendid drama.

As F. W. Dobbs-Allsopp has emphasized in another literary context, the poetic expression of profound existential grief is able to at least provide coherence and meaning, if not comfort or solace, to that grief.[29] For, as the Chorus sings in *The Women of Troy*,

> In times of sorrow it is a comfort to lament,
> To shed tears, and find music that will voice our grief.[30]

24. See Euripides, "Iphigenia in Tauris" and "Iphigenia in Aulis."

25. See Euripides, "Hecuba," in *The Complete Greek Drama*, Vol. I, 818–19. This eloquent text, dealing with the sacrifice of Polyxena, might have resonances of earlier sacrifices of maidens to propitiate the gods or expiate transgressions of sacred laws.

26. *Judges* 11:29–40. Yahweh did not provide a substitute for Jephthah's unfortunate daughter. A comparison with the story of Abraham and Isaac might suggest that gender distinction makes quite a difference in the way the God of Israel deals with the cultic rite of human sacrifice.

27. See Freud, *Totem and Taboo* (1913) and *Moses and Monotheism* (1937).

28. Euripides, "Women of Troy," 90.

29. Dobbs-Allsopp, *Lamentations*.

30. "Women of Troy," 110.

A View from Below

Yes, indeed. But, alas, the poetic dirge also aggravates and deepens the afflictions. It reawakens the experienced nightmares.[31] Hecuba, Priam's widow and Hector's mother, former queen of Troy, and now allotted to be a slave of Odysseus, the Greek general most disdained by the Trojan aristocracy, for he is a tricky deceiver, a master of lies, and weaver of fatal wiles, takes the lead by uttering a profoundly sad and heartrending expression of grief:

> I mourn for my dead world, my burning town,
> My sons, my husband, gone, all gone! . . .
> Now shrunk to nothing, sunk in mean oblivion!
>
> How must I deal with grief? . . .
> For those whom Fate has cursed
> Music itself sings but one note—
> Unending miseries, torment and wrong![32]

Andromache, widow of Hector, will have to contemplate the assassination of her only child, Astyanax, and suffer the lordship of Neoptolemus, the son of Achilles. She is forced to serve the murderer of her child, who is also the son of the warrior who killed her loved husband.

> To be dead is . . . better far than living on wretchedness.
> The dead feel nothing; evil then can cause no pain.
> But one who falls from happiness to unhappiness
> Wanders bewildered in a strange and hostile world.[33]

Andromache's body belongs now to the will of a hated man, who will dispose of it according to his whims and desires. For the rest of life, she will be a slave in a foreign land and a hostile house, devoid of any shred of hope of liberty or domestic happiness. During the days she will be subject to all kinds of exhausting toils, during the nights she will dread her master's lust.

> So I shall live a slave
> In the house of the very man who struck my husband dead.
> If I put from me my dear Hector's memory . . .
> I prove a traitor to the dead; but if I hate
> This man, I shall be hateful to my own master.[34]

---

31. See Dorfman, *Death and the Maiden*.
32. "Women of Troy," 93.
33. Ibid., 111.
34. Ibid., 112.

Both Hecuba and Andromache are burdened not only by the extreme misery to which they have fallen, but also by the absence of any meaningful hope for redemption. Any remembrance of past joys, in the alleys and gardens of lovely Troy, can only aggravate their present predicament. Any consideration of forthcoming events, as slaves ("a shadow of death—a slave!"[35]) in Ithaca, Athens, Sparta, or Argos, can only deepen their sufferings. There is no mental space for hope, for the imagination of a joyful and meaningful future.

Andromache laments the absolute impossibility of dreaming her liberation from abject servitude.

> For me there is not even
> The common refuge, hope. I cannot cheat myself
> With sweet delusions of some future happiness.[36]

A similar lament comes from the heart of Hecuba.

> Hope is dead; today I know
> The last throe of misery![37]

In another Euripides' drama, Polyxena, a young daughter of Priam and Hecuba, expresses analogous hopelessness. Odysseus has informed her of the tragic decision by the Greek army: that the maiden be sacrificed at Achilles' tomb, to honor the brave Achaean warrior. Polyxena rejects her mother's pleas and refuses to supplicate clemency. She prefers to die rather than live as a slave.

> Why should I prolong my days? . . . .
> Was I nursed . . . a maiden marked amid her fellows,
> equal to a goddess, save for death alone,
> but now a slave!
> That name first makes me long for death . . .
> No, never! Here I close my eyes upon the light
> Free as yet, and dedicate myself to Hades. . . .
> For I see naught within my reach to make me hope
> or expect with any confidence
> that I am ever again to be happy.[38]

---

35. Ibid., 96.
36. Ibid. 112
37. Ibid., 99.
38. "Hecuba," 814.

A View from Below

Those heartfelt woes, however, have to be expressed with utmost discretion, for, as slaves, they have lost the liberty to express openly their affliction or indignation. Their submission has to be complete, leaving no room even for their own inner selves. After hearing the horrifying news about the sentence of death decreed for her only child, Andromache is warned by the Greek messenger to accept her tragic fate in silence and submission.

> This too: don't call down
> Curses upon the Greeks. . . .
> If you are quiet . . .
> You'll find the Achaeans more considerate to yourself.[39]

CASSANDRA: FROM LAMENT TO DEFIANCE

Pain is thus mercilessly multiple: the death of the loved ones, the bondage of slavery, the extinction of hope, the masquerade of submission, and the silencing of lamentation and protest. Slavery, submission, hopelessness, simulation, silence: that is the cruel destiny of the captive Trojan women.

With one exception: Cassandra. A beautiful Trojan princess, a consecrated virgin to the altar of Apollo, Cassandra has been sacrilegiously chosen by Agamemnon as his slave and concubine, a toy for his lust and pleasure. Hecuba, her mother, is in pain for the fate of her daughter, compelled to serve the most implacable enemy of her city and people. Cassandra, however, fearlessly sings her disdain for the triumphant Achaeans, and intones a hymn in honor of the dead Trojan warriors.

> How different for the men of Troy, whose glory it was
> To die defending their own country! Those who fell
> Were carried back by comrades to their homes, prepared
> For burial by hands they loved, and laid to rest
> In the land that bore them . . . joys denied
> To the invaders.[40]

When her mother laments her lot ("A slave taken in war, a plunder of a conquering Greek"[41]), Cassandra, endowed by Apollo with prophetic powers, celebrates, not her submission, but the future catastrophe and tragedy of the house of Agamemnon, the cursed lineage of Atreus. She,

39. "Women of Troy," 114.
40. Ibid. 103.
41. Ibid. 102.

prophetess of doom, foresees the homicidal rage of Clytemnestra, who has not forgotten the sacrifice of Iphigenia and who will not forgive Agamemnon the introduction at her house of the young and beautiful Trojan, as his concubine. Cassandra's cries of woes mutate into resistance and defiance, vociferously singing and celebrating the assassination of Agamemnon, the oldest son of Atreus, by the hands of his own wife, an event that will transform his military victory into defeat and tragedy.

> Agamemnon,
> This famous king, shall find me a more fatal bride
> Than Helen. I shall kill him and destroy his house
> In vengeance for my brothers' and my father's death. . . .
> My bridal-bed promises death to my worst enemy . . .
>
> At the porch of death my bridegroom waits for me.
> Great chief of the Hellenes, fleeting shadow of magnificence,
> Your accursed life shall sink in darkness to an accursed grave . . .
>
> I will come triumphant to the house of Death,
> When I have brought to ruin the sons of Atreus, who destroyed us.[42]

She is the only captive Trojan woman who is able to metamorphose her misery and slavery into defiance and resistance. As her sister Polyxena, Cassandra willingly accepts her premature and violent death as unavoidable destiny. But, in a unique way, she is also able to deny her captors any honor and rejoices in the tragic reversal of destiny that awaits the Argive royal house. She calls forth the inner strength, the unconquerable pathos, able to reject the iron logic of war by assuming and accepting in her own self the death and sacrifice entailed by that logic. Cassandra is graced by a feminine fortitude and bravery sometimes unperceived by readers who, like Simone Weil, are fascinated by the seductive and poetic male heroism of the *Iliad*.

Thus Euripides, in a very different way from Aristophanes' delicious comedy "Lysistrata,"[43] not only gives voice to women's sufferings and lamentations as ominous consequences of war, but also foregrounds, in the character of Cassandra,[44] female defiance and resistance to violence and

---

42. Ibid., 102–105.

43. Aristophanes, "Lysistrata," Vol. II, 803–60. This is the literary source of that famous anti-war slogan: "Make love, not war!"

44. Similar resistance and defiance are also expressed by Andromache's fierce

destruction. Thus, early in the origins of our cultural and historical awareness, in the creative period between Homer and Euripides, the vast dramatic canvas of war and affliction, violence and defiance, military oppression and obstinate resistance is magnificently displayed. We can admire the courage of the ill-fated Hector and Achilles, yet share as well the afflictions of Hecuba and Andromache, marvel at the dignity of Polyxena's choice of death rather than slavery, and rejoice in the resistance and defiance of Cassandra under the sinister shadows of war and death.

GRIEVING BETWEEN BURKAS AND BOMBS

"The whole *Iliad* is overshadowed by the greatest of griefs that can come among men; the destruction of a city."[45] Thus Simone Weil summarizes the tragic drama of the most famous Hellenic epic poem. In the beginning there was war. Yes indeed, and throughout the entire human history, cities have been destroyed and lamentations have been uttered to express the profound afflictions entailed by such catastrophes. The pathos of war has too frequently defeated the ethos of peace. The biblical lament over the devastated Jerusalem echoes the agonies of the dwellers of many other destroyed cities:

> Jerusalem remembers
> in the days of her affliction and
> wandering...
> When her people fell into the hand
> of the foe....
> My eyes flow with rivers of tears
> because of the destruction of
> my people.[46]

Of all the afflictions narrated by the anonymous Hebrew poet, the most heartrending are the descriptions of the agony of the women survivors of the catastrophe, who face the horrifying temptation of maternal cannibalism.

> Should women eat their offspring,
> the children they have borne?...

---

confrontation with Menelaus, in the play that bears as title the name of the unfortunate Trojan widow, forced to be the slave and concubine of Neoptolemus, her husband's slayer. Euripides, "Andromache," Vol. I, 843–78.

45. "*Iliad*, Poem of Might," 178.
46. *Lamentations* 1:7; 3:48.

> The hands of compassionate women
> have boiled their own children:
> they became their food
> in the destruction of my people.[47]

During the last century, the strategic understanding of war as a conflict between nations, and not only between armies, coupled with the awesome development in military technology, has made cities a choice target of attack and destruction. Picasso's Guernica is the artistic symbol, as Hiroshima the painful living incarnation, of the transmogrification of the city, in times of war, from a place of human fulfillment into a Dantean metaphor of hell. Guernica, Dresden, Hiroshima, Groznyy, Sarajevo, Kabul, Baghdad, among many other cities, have witnessed stories of affliction similar to the woes uttered in the biblical *Lamentations* or in Euripides' "Women of Troy."

Women's woes of war and their resistance against the perennial proclivity to make force the arbiter of human conflicts, have come out from the margins of history and are now in the core of the early twenty-first century labors to forge a more humane and less violent world.[48] In many different languages and cultural contexts, the sad and defiant cries to God of contemporary Hecubas, Andromechas, or Cassandras have been vociferously expressed, in lamentation and protest for the ominous divine silence and absence, enacting once more the dramatic biblical voice of grief,

> I am one who has seen affliction
> under the rod of God's wrath...
> Though I call and cry for help,
> he shuts out my prayer...
> does the Lord not see it?[49]

Classical Greek literature springs from aristocratic sources. Homer's *Iliad* and Euripides plays are stories of the fateful and tragic endeavors of noble and aristocratic protagonists. Achilles, Hector, and Agamemnon are neither peasants nor laborers. They are of kingly ancestry. Hecuba, Andromache, Polyxena, and Cassandra lament their drastic reversal of fortune, from royal comfort to misery and servitude. Aristocracy matters here. As the chorus of one of Euripides' dramas affirms:

---

47. *Lamentations* 2:20; 4:10.

48. See Mostov, "'Our Women'/'Their Women,'" 515–29 and Boulding, "Feminist Inventions in the Art of Peacemaking," 408–38.

49. *Lamentations* 3:1, 8, 36.

A View from Below

> Oh! To have never been born,
> or sprung from noble sires,
> the heir to mansions richly stored . . .
> there is honour and glory for them
> when they are proclaimed scions
> of illustrious lines . . .[50]

A more popular, more inclusive, and less aristocratic consideration of violence and afflictions is indispensable today in our analysis of the woes of women enmeshed in war. If we truly strive to understand intellectually and share emotionally the sufferings and travails of so many women in ill-fated places like Afghanistan and Iraq, plagued by the violence of native tyrants and foreign invaders, their lives and liberties threatened by burkas and bombs, we must extend the horizon of our outlook to include and highlight those devoid of noble lineage and of wealth. In desperation and defiance, today's women voice their bitter lament as the female chorus in T. S. Eliot's *Murder in the Cathedral*:

> We know of oppression and torture,
> We know of extortion and violence,
> Destitution, disease,
> The old without fire in winter,
> The child without milk in summer,
> Our labour taken away from us,
> Our sins made heavier upon us.
> We have seen the young man mutilated,
> The torn girl trembling by the mill-stream.
> And meanwhile we have gone on living . . .
> Picking together the pieces . . .
> For sleeping, and eating and drinking and laughter[51]

An international humanitarian worker has thus assessed the new situation of women in "liberated" Afghanistan: "During the Taliban era if a woman went to market and showed an inch of flesh she would have been flogged, now she's raped."[52] Emerging from the margins of political or social power, in times of preventive and preemptive wars declared by mighty nations against weaker adversaries, the women of conflict-torn places like

---

50. "Andromache," 865.
51. "Murder in the Cathedral," 195.
52. Amnesty International, "Afghanistan. 'No one listens to us and no one treats us as human beings': Justice denied to Women." AI Index: ASA 11/023/2003 (October 6, 2003) 18.

Afghanistan and Iraq cry to God and to their fellow human beings for compassion and solidarity, for the recognition and restoration of their wounded and battered humanity.

The plight and woes of women in war are now being tragically replicated throughout Western Sudan, in the area of Darfur, where the female members of several ethnic groups suffer violence, abduction, rape, and sexual abuse by paramilitary groups, the so-called "Janjawid."[53] The plight, endurance, and hope of oppressed Islamic women cry out to us in the powerful and painful texts of the Egyptian writer Nawal El Saadawi. In her novels and feminist treatises, El Saadawi has given eloquent voice to the struggles of women in Islamic societies to shape their own destiny between the burkas and the bombs, to free themselves from the dominion of priests and warriors who in the name of God or war try to possess and control female existence.[54] Her writing "smiles the smile of a woman who has lost everything and kept her soul . . . Her suffering shows in the furrows of her face, but her eyes continue to shine with an inner glow."[55]

"No one listens to us and no one treats us as human beings,"[56] is the bitter and defiant protest of so many women who confront with dignity and courage the mullahs who want to confine and constrain their body and spirit and the imperial political leaders who blindly think that bombs are the best solution for today's complex global problems. It is our sacred duty and ethical responsibility to hear in contrition and commitment their clamors for justice and solidarity.[57]

Many of us received with joy and celebration the news that Shirin Ebadi, the Iranian judge and defender of the rights of women and children in the Islamic world, was granted the 2003 Peace Noble Prize. Judge Ebadi is a courageous woman who for many years has given vibrant voice to the woes and aspirations of so many of her Islamic sisters.[58] She has also denounced with eloquence and intelligence the actions of those governments who under the guise of a cosmic and mythic "war against terror" invade

53. See Amnesty International, "Sudan, Darfur. Rape as a weapon of war: Sexual violence and its consequences." AI Index AFR 54/076/2004 (19 July 2004).

54. See, for example, her novel *Fall of the Imam* and her literary self-portrait *Walking Through Fire: A Life of Nawal El Saadawi*.

55. *Fall of the Imam*, 24.

56. Amnesty International, "Afghanistan," 25.

57. For a female perspective on war and peace, see Boulding, *Cultures of Peace* and Pascual Morán, *Acción civil noviolenta: fuerza de espíritu, fuerza de paz*.

58. Ebadi, *History and documentation of human rights in Iran*.

nations, curtail civil liberties, and treat with disdain and cruelty those who dare to resist, sending them to twenty-first century gulags, like the U.S. military prisons in Guantánamo, Abu Ghraib, and nameless others in Afghanistan, veritable black holes where humans rights acknowledged and proclaimed by modern international law are so frequently forgotten and transgressed.[59]

Yes, indeed, but what about the bewildering dissonance between our duties as citizens, usually prescribed by those whose power enable them to define today's historical conflicts in terms of national might, profit, and prestige, and Dietrich Bonhöffer's ethical demand "to see the great events of history from below, from the perspective of the outcast, the suspects, the maltreated, the powerless, the oppressed, the reviled—in short, from the perspective of those who suffer"?[60] This, doubtless, is the intellectual and moral dilemma faced by American citizens today, in an environment so redolent of chauvinism and jingoism, who cannot however evade, and do not desire to elude, the challenges coming "from below," from the woes of women in Islamic societies, trapped between burkas and bombs, between the religious power of the authoritarian mullahs and the military aggressiveness of the United States government, women whose woes mutate from lament to defiance to resistance.

What are we to say in such a historical context? It might be true, as Susan Sontag has recently written, that "most people will not question the rationalizations offered by their government for starting or continuing a war."[61] Indeed, but not all people and not at all times. Almost five decades ago, a young African American writer, James Baldwin, raised in the bitter streets of Harlem, and wrestling with the conflict between his national identity and his quest for human justice, laid down an insightful principle that deserves to be the last sentence of this essay: "I love America more than any other country in the world, and, exactly for this reason, I insist on the right to criticize her perpetually."[62]

---

59. Danner, *Torture and Truth*.
60. Bonhöffer, *Letters and Papers from Prison*, 16.
61. Sontag, *Regarding the Pain of Others*, 38.
62. Baldwin, *Notes of a Native Son*, 9.

3

Listening and Engaging the Voices from the Margins
Postcolonial Observations from the Caribbean[1]

> We have for once learnt to see the great events of world history from below, from the perspective of the outcast, the suspects, the maltreated, the powerless, the oppressed, the reviled—in short, from the perspective of those who suffer.
>
> —Dietrich Bonhöffer[2]

POSTCOLONIAL THEORY IN A COLONIAL SITUATION

The organizers of this 2013 Lutheran Bishops Academy have invited me to speak about "Listening and Engaging the Voices from the Margin: Postcolonial Observations from the Caribbean." I find this invitation rather perplexing, for I originate from Puerto Rico, a Caribbean island that has been aptly described by one of our foremost juridical scholars as "the oldest

---

[1] 'First lecture delivered to the Evangelical Lutheran Church in America's Bishops Academy, January 3, 2013, in San Juan, Puerto Rico.

[2] Bonhöffer, *Letters and Papers from Prison*, 16

colony of the world."³ Christopher Columbus claimed possession of the island for the crown of Castile in 1493 and, after the defeat of a desperate native insurrection during the second decade of the sixteenth century, it remained part of the Spanish empire till 1898, when it was conquered by the United States.

The transfer of sovereignty from Madrid to Washington was accomplished through the two classical ways of solving conflicts among powerful nations: war and diplomacy. War was perpetrated in the tropical Caribbean and the Philippines; diplomacy was negotiated later in elegant and cosmopolitan Paris.⁴ No need to consult the natives. Washington, Madrid, and Paris were the sites of privileged historical agency. In early 1898 Puerto Rico was a Spanish colony; at the end of that fateful year, it had become a colony of the United States. These were the initial stages of imperial *pax americana*. It was part and parcel of the Age of Empire, so aptly named by the British historian Eric Hobsbawm.⁵ From the Philippines and Guam, in the Pacific, to Cuba and Puerto Rico, in the Caribbean, the American ideology of manifest destiny, with its strong religious undertones, was transgressing national boundaries.

> By 1899, the United States had forged a new empire. American politicians, naval officers, and businessmen had created it amid much debate and with conscious purpose. The empire expanded from the continental frontier, as defined by Frederick Jackson Turner, to preeminence in the Western Hemisphere, and, for good or ill, into the farthest reaches of the Pacific.⁶

We have learnt much from Edward Said, Homi Bhabha, Gayatry Spivak, and Walter Mignolo about *colonial discourse* and postcolonial critique.⁷ Even before these four distinguished émigrés, there were the crucial analyses of colonial ideology and mentality drafted by Franz Fanon and

---

3. Trías Monge, *Puerto Rico*.

4. The war between the United States and Spain concluded with the Treaty of Paris, signed December 10, 1898. Spain, militarily defeated, was forced to relinquish its dominion over the Philippines, Cuba, Guam, and Puerto Rico to the new American colossus. García Martínez, *Libro rojo/Tratado de París*.

5. Hobsbawm, *Age of Empire*.

6. Musicant, *Empire By Default*, 658.

7. Said, *Culture and Imperialism*; Bhabha, *Location of Culture*; Spivak, *In Other Worlds*; Mignolo, *Darker Side of the Renaissance*.

Albert Memmi.[8] Also, the critical examination of the strategies of coloniality—military power, economic domination, racial hierarchy, cultural arrogance—by the Peruvian Aníbal Quijano.[9] Colonized subjects providing theoretical paradigms to their colonizers? Dislocated, "out of place"[10] Third World intellectuals providing academic lessons to the masters of the world? Quite a paradox of these postcolonial times!

Colonial discourse mystifies imperial dominion. It crafts by persuasion what the mechanisms of coercion are unable to achieve: the fine-tuned consent and admiration of the colonized subjects. It diffuses and affirms imperial, ideological hegemony. Its greatest creation is what V. S. Naipaul has called *mimic men*.[11] When the U. S. troops invaded Puerto Rico, their commanding general, Nelson Appleton Miles, of notorious reputation due to his participation in the Wounded Knee massacre, made the following proclamation "to the Inhabitants of Porto [sic] Rico":

> In the prosecution of the war against the Kingdom of Spain by the people of the United States, in the cause of liberty, justice, and humanity, its military forces have come to occupy the island of Puerto Rico. They come bearing the banner of Freedom . . .
> We have come to promote your prosperity and bestow upon you the . . . blessings of the liberal institutions of our government . . . the advantages and blessings of enlightened civilization.[12]

In 1493, and more firmly in 1508, the Spaniards came to Puerto Rico with the proclaimed purpose of converting its idolatrous inhabitants to the one and only true religion, Christianity, and to teach them how to live according to the European ethical norms of a civil and ordered society. In 1898, the Americans came to impart upon us, poor tropical barbarians, the blessings of liberty, justice, humanity, and enlightened civilization. To crown its generosity, in 1917, without consulting "the Inhabitants of *Porto Rico*" (again, who cares about the views and feelings of colonized subjects?), Washington bestowed upon us the gift of American citizenship. That

---

8. Fanon, *Wretched of the Earth*; Memmi, *Colonizer and the Colonized*.

9. Quijano, "Colonialidad del poder, cultura y conocimiento en América Latina," 113–121; Quijano, "The Colonial Nature of Power and Latin America's Cultural Experience," 27–38; and Quijano, "Coloniality of Power, Eurocentrism, and Latin America," 533–580.

10. Said, *Out of Place*.

11. Naipaul, *Mimic Men*.

12. Miles, *Serving the Republic*, 301–2.

citizenship has allowed our people to participate in the military adventures of Washington to extend its "empire of freedom," from the trenches of the First World War to the streets of Kabul and Baghdad. As an added bonus, we do not need to mess with any of the crucial decisions regarding our political condition and fate. We can rest assured that those decisions, usually important dimensions of democratic sovereignty, are well taken care by the wisdom and benevolence of the powers that be in Washington. How fortunately colonial we Puerto Ricans have been!

If we are going to converse seriously about postcolonial perspectives for theology and the church in the public square, let us first be aware of the delightful irony that I, a colonized subject, have been invited to talk about "religion, politics, and empire, from the margins" to citizens of the empire that rules over my people! Maybe this is another occasion to reiterate Gayatri Spivak's famous query, "can the subaltern speak?" A question that Edward Said dared to answer affirmatively: "Indeed, the subaltern *can* speak, as the history of liberation movements in the twentieth century eloquently attests."[13]

COLONIALITY AND DIASPORA

To the ambivalence of a postcolonial colony, whose residents as citizens of the empire can claim in the courts the civil liberties of their citizenship but not its political rights, we should add the crucial fact that more than half of the Puerto Rican population resides in mainland United States.[14] Legally, those Puerto Ricans are not migrants. Psychologically and culturally, they are. They belong to the history of modern diasporas. And diasporas are the source of the bewildering multiculturalism of the postmodern mega cities.

Migration and diaspora are crucial dimensions of Puerto Rico's modern history.[15] They constitute an experience shared by many former and present colonial peoples all over the world. Nowadays they have also become important themes of conversation in postcolonial cultural studies.[16] But, as Homi Bhabha has stressed, diaspora is an important object of

13. Spivak, "Can the Subaltern Speak?," 271–313; Said, *Orientalism*, 335.
14. Falcón, *Atlas of Stateside Puerto Ricans*.
15. As Princeton University professor Arcadio Díaz-Quiñones has beautifully shown, in his book *El arte de bregar*, Puerto Rican culture cannot be genuinely assessed if the creativity of its diaspora community is neglected or its significance diminished.
16. Barkan and Shelton, *Borders, Exiles, Diasporas*.

critical analysis because it is the sociohistorical existential context of many displaced Third World peoples: "For the demography of the new internationalism is the history of postcolonial migration, the narratives of cultural and political diaspora . . . the poetics of exile . . ."[17]

Diaspora entails dislocation, displacement, but also a painful and complex process of forging new strategies to articulate cultural differences and identifications. In the Western cosmopolis, with its heterogeneous and frequently conflicting ethnocultural minorities that belie the mythical *e pluribus unum*, the émigré exists in ambivalent tension. More than half a century ago, Franz Fanon brilliantly described the peculiar gaze of so many white French people at the growing presence of Black Africans and Caribbeans in their national midst.[18] Scorn and fear are entwined in that stare. The diasporic person frequently feels, alas, "like a man without a passport who is turned away from every harbour," the anguished dread that haunts the persecuted whisky priest of Graham Greene's magnificent novel, *The Power and the Glory*.[19]

Frequently, nostalgia grips his or her soul, in the beautiful words of a biblical lamentation:

> By the rivers of Babylon -
> there we sat down and there we wept
> when we remembered Zion.
>
> . . .
>
> How could we sing the Lord's
> song in foreign land
>
> (Psalm 137:1, 4, NRSV)

Often, however, and sometimes simultaneously, the displacement of migration creates a new a space of liberation from the atavistic constraints and bondages of the native cultural community and opens new vistas, perspectives, and horizons. To repressed persons, exile in a metropolis like London, Paris, or New York could convey an expansion of individual autonomy, even if its sinister hidden side might turn out to be despair or death.[20] Diasporic existence, as Bhabha has so forcefully reiterated,

---

17. Bhabha, *Location of Culture*, 5.
18. Fanon, *Peau Noir, Masques Blancs*.
19. Greene, *Power and the Glory*, 102.
20. This was the case for two creative Caribbean writers, marginalized and despised in their homelands, the Cuban Reinaldo Arenas and the Puerto Rican Manuel Ramos-Otero, who found in New York a wider horizon for their literary talents, a greater realm

questions fixed and static notions of cultural and communal identity. In the diaspora, identity is not conceived as a pure essence to be nostalgically preserved, but as an emancipatory project to be fashioned, in an alien territory, in a foreign language, as a polyphonic process of creative imagination. In many instances, yet, "the restoration of a collective sense of identity and historical agency in the home country may well be mediated through the diaspora."[21]

As Walter Mignolo has so provocatively asserted,[22] diaspora, as a site of critical enunciation, compels the rethinking of the geopolitical distinction, so dear to many Third World thinkers, between center and periphery, and elicits a border thinking that changes not only the content, but also the terms of the intellectual global dialogue. The émigré's cultural differences produce subaltern significations that resist the cultural cannibalism of the metropolitan melting pot. Diasporic communities are, to quote once more Bhabha, "wandering peoples who will not be contained within the *Heim* of the national culture and its unisonant discourse, but are themselves the marks of a shifting boundary that alienates the frontiers of the modern nation."[23]

The existential dislocation of diaspora, its cultural hybridity, recreates the complex intertwined ethnic and racial sources of many migrant communities. Asked to whom does she owe allegiance, Clare, the Jamaican protagonist of Michelle Cliff's novel *No Telephone to Heaven*, replies: "I have African, English, Carib in me."[24] She is a mestiza moving between Kingston, New York, and London, searching for a place to call home, torn between the quest for solidarity in the forging of a common identity and the lure of solitude in a strange land. To be part of a pilgrim diaspora is a difficult and complex challenge, which, to avoid utopian illusions, must be faced having in mind the superb irony of that master of twentieth-century skepticism, himself a displaced wanderer, James Joyce: "We were always loyal to lost causes . . . Success is for us the death of the intellect and of the imagination."[25]

---

of personal freedom, but also AIDS-related death. See Ríos-Avila, "Caribbean Dislocations," 101–22.

21. Elazar Barkan and Marie-Denise Shelton, "Introduction," *Borders, Exiles, Diasporas*, 5.

22. Mignolo, *Local Histories/Global Designs*.

23. *Location of Culture*, 164.

24. Cliff, *No Telephone to Heaven*, 189.

25. Joyce, *Ulysses*, 131.

Essays from the Margins

From the margins of empires and metropolitan centers of powers, the crossroads of borders and frontiers, in the proximity of so many different and frequently conflictive cultural worlds, in the maelstroms of the global mega cities and the virtual imagined communities of the internet, arise constantly new challenges to the international structures of power and control.[26] There colonial discourses meet their nemesis: postcolonial defiance. In the ecumenicity of diaspora, to quote again Bhabha, "we must not change merely the narratives of our histories, but transform our sense of what it means to live, to be, in other times and different places, both human and historical."[27]

It is usually there, in the counter invasion of the "others," the colonized barbarians, into the realms of the lords of the world that the silenced peoples find the sonority of their voices and reconfigure their historical sagas into meaningful human stories. The quasi-beastly shadows of *Heart of Darkness* dare to disrupt the imperial monologue. They hybridize the language of the colonizers to reshape and narrate their own histories. As Chinua Achebe, engaged in a critical dialogue with the specter of Joseph Conrad, so eloquently has written in a text significantly titled *Home and Exile*, "My hope for the twenty-first [century] is that it will see the first fruits . . . of the process of 're-storying' peoples who had been knocked silent by the trauma of all kinds of dispossession."[28]

For the early Christian communities, diaspora was a constant perspective in their way of living and understanding their faith, as expressed in a letter written by an anonymous Christian author in the second or third century: "They [Christians] take part in everything like citizens, and endure everything like aliens. Every foreign country is their native land, and every native land a foreign country."[29] The Bible itself, as a canonic sacred text, is a literary creature of the diaspora,[30] for the Old Testament was born from the sufferings of the dispersed Hebrew nation and the New Testament was written in the koine Greek, the lingua franca of many diasporic peoples of the Hellenistic age. The New Testament faith is, in many ways, a devout endless wandering, by a community of "aliens and exiles" (I Peter 2:11), to the unreachable ends of the world and ends of times, in search of God

26. Hardt and Negri, *Multitude*.
27. *Location of Culture*, 256.
28. Achebe, *Home and Exile*, 79.
29. "Address to Diognetus," 278.
30. Smith-Christopher, *Biblical Theology of Exile*.

and human solidarity. The concept of diaspora could thus be a significant crossroad of encounter, a dialectical hinge, between postcolonial cultural studies and theological hermeneutics.[31]

Puerto Ricans constitute an important part of the US Latino/Hispanic population, that sector of the American society whose growth, in the view of many, enriches multicultural diversity, but has also led Samuel P. Huntington to warn that it constitutes a "major potential threat to the cultural and possibly political integrity of the United States."[32] How interesting that the former prophet of the "clash of civilizations," beyond the frontiers of the American colossus, became the apostle of the "clash of cultures," within its borders. According to this eminent Harvard professor, the main problem of Latino/Hispanics is not the illegality in which many of them incur to reside in the US, but the threat they represent to the American national identity and its allegedly traditional "Anglo-Protestant" culture.

In that clash of cultures, we Puerto Ricans are distinguished warriors. We excel in the "double consciousness," the transculturation, and the border thinking that Walter Mignolo has so suggestively rescued from the African American W. E. B. Dubois, the Cuban Fernando Ortiz, and the Chicana Gloria Anzaldúa. In Puerto Rico, we take delight in our Spanish language, in the mainland we share the linguistic fate of the diaspora, we experience "the pain and perverse pleasure of writing in a second language," in the words of that exceptional Haitian scholar Michel-Rolph Trouillot.[33] The experience of *heteroglossia* (Bakhtin), of thinking, speaking, and writing in a different language, opens unexpected spaces for a heterodox understanding of the hybridizing encounters of peoples and cultures.

The colonial situation, encompassing its ensuing cultural symbiosis, its political and juridical dissolution, and the persisting socioeconomic inequities, constitute the historical matrix of many modern diasporas and, thus, a crucial source of the multicultural collisions in the imperial metropolitan centers. In the words of William Schweiker, University of Chicago professor of theological ethics,

> International cities are a 'place' in which people's identities, sense of self, others, and the wider world, as well as values and desires, are locally situated but altered by global dynamics . . . The compression of the world found in massive cities is thus a boon for

31. Krüger, *La diáspora*.
32. Huntington, *Who Are We*, 243.
33. Trouillot, *Silencing the Past*, xv.

the formation of new self-understandings, especially for dislocated peoples . . . This is especially pointed when those 'others' are implicated in histories of suffering. The compression of the world confronts us with the problem of how to live amid others, even enemies.³⁴

In the borderlands a new poetic of political resistance is developed, as the late Gloria Anzaldúa so hauntingly perceived:

> In the Borderlands
> you are the battleground
> where enemies are kin to each other;
> you are at home, a stranger . . .
> To survive in the Borderlands
> you must live *sin fronteras*
> be a crossroads.³⁵

The postmodern and postcolonial mega cities compress times and spaces into borderlands of cultures, religiosities, traditions, and values. There it is impossible to evade the gaze of the others, and the primordial biblical question—"am I my brother's keeper?"—acquires new connotations and urgency. A new sensitivity has to be forged to the rendering ambivalences, the sorrows and joys, of diasporic existence of the peoples who live day and night with the uncanny feeling of existing as Gentile aliens within the gates of holy Jerusalem.

THEOLOGY AND POSTCOLONIAL STUDIES: A CRITICAL OBSERVATION

It is not surprising that Bible scholars—Stephen D. Moore, Fernando Segovia, R. S. Sugistharajah, Musa Dube, Roland Boer, and Richard Horsley, among others—have been first and foremost among the theological disciplines to pay close attention to postcolonial theories.³⁶ After all, it is impossible to evade the pervasive ubiquity of empires, imperial conquests,

---

34. Schweiker, *Theological Ethics and Global Dynamics*, 6–7.

35. Anzaldúa, *Borderlands/La Frontera*, 216–17.

36. Moore and Segovia, *Postcolonial Biblical Criticism*; Sugirtharajah, *Postcolonial Bible*; Sugirtharajah, *Postcolonial Criticism and Biblical Interpretation*; Sugirtharajah, *Postcolonial Biblical Reader*; Boer, *Postcolonialism and the Hebrew Bible*; Dube, *Postcolonial Feminist Interpretation of the Bible*; Horsley, *Jesus and Empire*; Horsley, *Paul and Empire*; and Horsley, *Paul and the Roman Imperial Order*.

and anti-colonial resistances in the Jewish-Christian sacred Scriptures. The geopolitical expansions or contractions of the Egyptian, Chaldean, Assyrian, Persian, Macedonian, and Roman empires constitute the main historical landscape of the entire biblical corpus.

From the Exodus saga to the anti-Roman apocalyptic visions of *Revelation*[37] only a fruitless strategy of hermeneutical evasion would be able to suppress the importance of imperial hegemony in the configuration of human existence and religious faith in the Bible. Even a comprehensive study of gender and sex in the Bible has to take into consideration the different ways in which Esther and Judith use their female sexuality in critical historical instances in which the fate of the children of Abraham is at the stake of a powerful empire. How to forget that Jesus was executed by the Roman authorities as a political subversive? Any theory of atonement that elides the intense political drama of the last days of Jesus transforms it into an abstract unhistorical dogma, or in a display of tasteless masochism à la Mel Gibson's *The Passion of the Christ* (2004).

Thus, it was to be expected that biblical scholars would be the first in the academic fields of religious studies to incorporate the emphases on geopolitical hegemony and resistance provided by postcolonial theories to the array of other contemporary hermeneutical perspectives. The question raised by R. S. Sugirtharajah, however, is poignant indeed:

> One of the weighty contributions of postcolonial criticism has been to put issues relating to colonialism and imperialism at the center of critical and intellectual inquiry . . . What is striking about systematic theology is the reluctance of its practitioners to address the relation between European colonialism and the field. There has been a marked hesitancy to critically evaluate the impact of the empire among systematic theologians.[38]

To be fair, some theologians are beginning to awake from their disciplinary slumber to take into serious consideration the crucial issues of geopolitical power. Creative theologians, like Catherine Keller, Mark Lewis Taylor, Kwok Pui-lan, Wonhee Anne Joh, Mayra Rivera, Joerg Rieger, and others, have begun to face with intellectual rigor and rhetorical elegance the challenges raised by postcolonial studies and dialogues.[39] For those

---

37. Libânio e Bingemer, *Escatologia Cristã*; Richard, *Apocalipsis*; Blount, *Can I Get a Witness?*

38. Sugirtharajah, "Complacencies and Cul-de-sacs," 22.

39. Keller, *God and Power*; Taylor, *Religion, Politics, and the Christian Righ*; Kwok,

studies and dialogues, the Caribbean, just where I happen to live and work, might be the best place to start.

Let me explain this last statement that many of you might find rather perplexing. Fernando Segovia has written a precise and concise exposition of the convergence between biblical scholarship and postcolonial studies.[40] Never an uncritical reader, Segovia raises several poignant critiques of the latter. Two of them are particularly relevant to the argument I want to develop: First, the lack of attention, by most postcolonial intellectuals, to the Latin American and Caribbean Iberian imperial formations as they developed between the end of the fifteenth century and the first decades of the seventeenth.[41] Second, the scarcity of analysis of religion as a crucial dimension of the imperial-colonial ideological frameworks. To quote Segovia on this second issue:

> It is almost as if religious texts and expressions did not form part of the cultural production and as if religious institutions and practices did not belong to the social matrix of imperial-colonial frameworks. I would argue . . . that religion is to be acknowledged and theorized as a constitutive component of such frameworks, and a most important one . . .[42]

The existential relevance of both issues for Segovia, a Cuban-born person who describes himself as "a student of religion in general and of the Christian faith in particular," seems obvious. I, as another Caribbean-born student of religion and theological ideas, share both concerns.

It is hard to deny that Segovia is *partially* right, for he is referring to the postcolonial cultural studies as they emerged from the twilight of the European empires that developed in the wake of the Enlightenment. What has been named by an eminent British historian the classic age of Empire[43] is the basic matrix whence the critical texts of Said, Bhabha and Spivak emerge. Even a very useful introductory text in the field, *Post-Colonial Studies: The Key Concepts*, edited by Ashcroft, Griffiths and Tiffin, proceeds as if the sixteenth-century Iberian empires never existed or as if religious

---

Postcolonial Imagination and Feminist Theology; Joh, *Heart of the Cros*; Rieger, *Christ & Empire*; Keller, Nausner, and Rivera, *Postcolonial Theologies*.

40. Segovia, "Mapping the Postcolonial Optic," 23–78.
41. Ibid., 73.
42. Ibid., 74–75.
43. Hobsbawm, *Age of Empire*.

Listening and Engaging the Voices from the Margins

discourses have never been used as motivation for conquest and colonization.[44] The end result of those analytical occlusions is the homogenization of imperial experiences and, therefore, of colonial defiance.[45]

In many postcolonial texts we learn a lot about the multifarious resonances of the notorious 1835 Macaulay's Minute on Indian Education, but almost nothing about the intense theological controversies, juridical disputes and philosophical debates (Francisco de Vitoria, Bartolomé de las Casas, Juan Ginés de Sepúlveda, José de Acosta) during the sixteenth-century Spanish conquest of the Americas, despite the fact that they anticipate most of the latter colonial and anti-colonial discourses.[46] The discussion by Vitoria about the justice of the wars against the Native Americans foreshadows all posterior arguments on the legitimacy of imperial wars.[47] The dispute between Las Casas and Sepúlveda about the rationality of the Native Americans and the adequacy of conversion by conquest inaugurates a long series of similar latter debates.[48] The lengthy treatise of Acosta on the Christianization and civilization of the American "barbarians" is paragon of subsequent analogous imperial justifications.[49]

Segovia is therefore right in his critique to the mainstream postcolonial studies. Yet, his critique reiterates that same mistake. He also excludes from the rather porous and vague boundaries of postcolonial studies authors that

44. Ashcroft, Griffiths, and Tiffin, *Post-Colonial Studies*. Sometimes their disregard for the sixteenth-century imperial formations leads them into egregious mistakes, like asserting that "in 1503, Bishop Las Casas . . . proposed . . . systematic importation of blacks" as "an alternative to indigenous labor" (ibid. 212). In 1503 Bartolomé de Las Casas was not yet a bishop and he did not propose to bring Black slaves to the new Spanish territories till the middle of the second decade of that century. See Rivera-Pagán, *A Violent Evangelism*, 180–95. See also Rivera-Pagán, "Freedom and Servitude," 316–62. Several of their statements regarding Latin America are not to be trusted—"the slave system . . . persisted in the Caribbean and some South American areas until the 1830s" (*Post-Colonial Studies*, 214)—whereas slavery was not abolished in Puerto Rico until 1873, in Cuba until 1886, and in Brazil until 1888, which shows the lack of attention of several postcolonial scholars to the colonial history of Latin America and the Spanish Caribbean.

45. Curiously, Chinua Achebe is mentioned once in Ashcroft, Griffiths, and Tiffin's textbook, but his 1958 classic novel, *Things Fall Apart*, one of the foremost literary assessments of the convergence between European colonization of African and Christian missions, is not even alluded to.

46. Dussel, *Política de la liberación*, 186–210.

47. Vitoria, "On the American Indians" (*De indis*, I), *Political Writings*, 231–92.

48. Las Casas, *In Defense of the Indians*.

49. Acosta, *De procuranda indorum salute* (2 vols.).

do in fact pay serious attention to both the Iberian sixteenth-century imperial formations and, as an unavoidable consequence, to the role of religious discourses in those geopolitical structures of control and dominion. The initial shaping of European global imperial expansion in Latin America and the Caribbean during the sixteenth century, in conjunction with the emergence of early modernity, capitalist accumulation, transatlantic slave trade, the proclamation of the Christian gospel as imperial ideology, and the othering of non-European peoples, have been topics of rigorous academic research and publications by two Argentinean émigrés, Walter Mignolo and Enrique Dussel.[50] Lewis Hanke[51] and Anthony Pagden[52] have also dealt extensively with that complex configuration of themes, engaging frequently in a comparative critical analysis with more recent empires.[53] I myself have scholarly engaged the theological debates that accompanied the emergence of the transatlantic Iberian empire in the sixteenth century.[54]

To expand the analytical horizon of the postcolonial discussion, let us briefly take a look at one of the first documents in which the European eyes gaze lustfully at overseas lands and peoples, the Caribbean where modern colonialism was initiated.

COLUMBUS AND THE RHETORICS OF POSSESSION

The last decades of the fifteenth century and the entire sixteenth were times of adventurous European overseas explorations. Ships from Portugal and Castile were constantly encountering exotics lands and strange peoples. Designing strategic plans for political dominion, economic enrichment, and religious mission required information. Epistles frequently provided that knowledge. They were the most expeditious way of conveying to the European ruling sectors the wondrous impressions of travelers, explorers, and conquerors. Cupidity for knowledge, gold, spices, and souls to redeem

---

50. Mignolo, *Darker Side of the Renaissance, Local Histories/Global Designs*; Mignolo, *Darker Side of Western Modernity*; Dussel, *Invention of the Americas*.

51. See Lewis Hanke's books: *Spanish Struggle for Justice*; *Aristotle and the American Indian*; and *All Mankind is One*.

52. The following important texts by Anthony Pagden can be consulted: *Fall of Natural Man*; *Spanish Imperialism and the Political Imagination*; and *Lords of all the World*.

53. Among theologians, Joerg Rieger is a distinguished exception. He devotes a chapter of one of his books to the critical analysis of Bartolomé de las Casas's Christology in the context of the sixteenth-century imperial expansion. *Christ & Empire*, 159–96.

54. Rivera-Pagán, *Violent Evangelism* and *Entre el oro y la fe*.

was the order of the day. The epistle was the door by which many of those recently found lands and communities were registered in European literary historiography. Paradoxically, for many of them, that literary inscription was also the source of their historical annihilation.

Many of those letters became the substratum of subsequent historical works, as was the case with Peter Martyr of Anghiera's *Decades of the New World*, which was built upon his correspondence with several highly placed Renaissance dignitaries. One of Amerigo Vespucci's epistles, the famed "novus mundus" text, was the peculiar source for the general name of the lands that we presently inhabit—America. Hernán Cortés's epistolary is still a model of the literary configuration of colonial conquest.[55] Significant traces of these epistles can be perceived in several key sixteenth-century works, such as Thomas More's *Utopia* or Montaigne's *Essays*. The dawn of modernity was accompanied by territorial expansion and a new literary passion.

A letter written by Christopher Columbus, on February 15, 1493,[56] was the first window of perception regarding the islands and peoples encountered during the four months he navigated through what is now called, thanks to one of his many linguistic confusions, the Caribbean. This brief epistle forged the first images of those lands and communities in the European Christian mentality. It is a founding text; a primal document that initiates a literature of imperialism. Columbus's letter shrewdly constructs a lasting vision of lands and peoples; it is one of the first instances of colonial discourse and imperial gaze.

Samuel Eliot Morison named it "The letter of Columbus announcing the discovery of America" and that title has become the traditional way of referring to it. A careful reading of the text, however, disturbs the certainty of the traditional title. First, the epistle never refers to "America"—Columbus simply writes that he had "reached the Indies" [219/7]. His "triumph," in his mind, is opening a new, convenient, and profitable route of navigation to the "Indies," not discovering a new continent. But, more

---

55. Martyr of Anghiera, *De orbe novo*, 2 vols.; Vespucio, *El Nuevo Mundo*, 171–195 (in Italian and Spanish), 295–306 (in English); Cortés, *Letters from Mexico* (1520-6).

56. "Carta a Luis de Santángel," 219-26; Columbus, *New and Fresh English Translation*, 7–16. I will cite Columbus's letter giving first the page number of the Varela/Gil edition and secondly the page number of the Morison translation. As John Boyd Thacher wrote in his biography of Columbus: "We know of no other work which in the short space of ten or twelve months at the close of the fifteenth century passed through thirteenth editions . . ." Thacher, *Christopher Columbus*, 72.

importantly, Columbus never uses the term "discovery" or the verb "discover." The concept of the "discovery of America" was a later invention, as Edmundo O'Gorman exhaustively demonstrated in his lengthy treatments of the subject.[57] The event has been named "discovery of America" as a way of beautifying its image (who can be against "discovering America"?) and simultaneously silencing its tragic dimensions.[58] Naming it "discovery" is nothing but a semantic asepsis of the event.

What does, therefore, Columbus want to narrate? "Sir . . . I reached the Indies . . . And there I found very many islands filled with people without number, and of them all, I have taken possession . . . of all I have taken possession for their Highnesses . . ." [219, 223/7, 12]. The letter does not narrate a discovery, but an *event of taking possession*. This, for Columbus, is the core of his enterprise: the act of taking possession of all the encountered lands and peoples. Stephen Greenblatt rightly terms Columbus's performance of taking possession a linguistic act, a discursive, scriptural operation. "For Columbus, taking possession is principally the performance of a set of linguistic acts: declaring, witnessing, recording."[59] Right, but we have to be more precise: It is a linguistic act that is not merely inscribed in a literary text—the epistle. It is also registered in the appropriate legal archive. It is a juridical linguistic act by means of which a formal declaration of legal appropriation is rendered. Columbus carefully registers the data he believes to encounter and perceive (much of it are monumental confusions) in a protocol with juridical, fateful consequences. As a juridical inscription, he is scrupulous inscribing that the proper ceremony has been performed—"by proclamation and with the royal standard displayed"—registering that nobody contradicted his act of taking possession—"and nobody objected" [219/7].

The literary act of taking possession is thus also a juridical linguistic act and a liturgical enactment, a ceremony, in which royal banners are displayed and some kind of religious ritual is performed (prayer, invocation of the divine name, erecting a cross), for it is in the name of God, and not only of Queen Isabella and King Ferdinand that the event takes place. Thus,

---

57. O'Gorman, *La idea del descubrimiento de América*. See also O'Gorman, *Invention of America*.

58. Trouillot, *Silencing the Past*, 114: "The naming of the 'fact' is itself a narrative of power disguised as innocence . . . To call 'discovery' the first invasions of inhabited lands by Europeans is an exercise in Eurocentric power that already frames future narratives of the event so described."

59. Greenblatt, *Marvelous Possessions*, 57.

at the beginning and the end of his epistle, Columbus expresses gratitude to "the eternal God, Our Lord," the author of "the great victory which has crowned" his expedition.[60] The text in which the possession of the encountered lands and peoples is narrated has a juridical dimension and a theological justification.

The Spanish scholar Francisco Morales Padrón has studied meticulously this issue. His main conclusion is valid: "Discovery was always followed by the act of taking possession," therefore, "discovery and conquest are part of one and the same process."[61] Morales Padrón, however, disregards an important dimension: every act of possessing is also an act of dispossessing. Yet, he correctly emphasizes that Columbus's acts of taking possession, as would be reaffirmed by Pope Alexander VI in his 1493 decrees regarding Iberian expansion overseas,[62] have a religious background. The lands have heathen princes, but such authorities do not posses authentic authority of sovereignty, thus the first Christian nation to encounter them has the theologico-juridical right to claim them. This principle will be disputed, in Vitoria's 1539 lecture on the wars against the "Indians" and in the 1551 Valladolid debate between Las Casas and Sepúlveda. But those later disputes were certainly not in the mind of Columbus while engaging in his possessing paroxysm.

If heathen lands are taken possession of, they have to be baptized. Christian baptism, let us not forget, traditionally implies the act of renaming. That is exactly what Columbus does. He baptizes and renames the lands he finds, for it would not be proper to register them with their infidel names. Christening the lands, Columbus exercises the power of naming and confers to them new Christian names. Thus they are inscribed in the European chronicles and archives with their Christian names, following both church dogma and royal sycophancy: "El Salvador," "Santa María de la Concepción," "Fernandina," "Isabela," "Juana." Greenblatt affirms that this "act [of naming] . . . is a cancellation of an existing name."[63] What in fact is erased is the faculty of the native inhabitants to name their place, as their authority to name their culture and deities will also soon be denied. The

---

60. Alejo Carpentier, who always wants to make fun of the Admiral, calls it ironically a "sacra reppresentazione." Carpentier, *El arpa y la sombra*, 160.

61. Morales Padrón, "Descubrimiento y toma de posesión," quotations from page 379 and 328.

62. Latin transcripts and English translations in Davenport, *European Treaties*, 56–83.

63. *Marvelous Possessions*, 82.

sacrament of baptism has traditionally contained a rite of exorcism: the protection of the baptized from the dominion of the demons. Demons will soon be called the native deities.

The letter proceeds to "describe" the lands and the people. Those descriptions would be their first inscriptions in European literature and would forge their initial construct in Western Christian imagination. Columbus's text becomes euphoric—the islands are a paradise: their beauty, splendor, and magnificence are unsurpassed. The possessed lands, the letter continues, also enjoy incomparable wealth. They contain immense resources of great value—cotton, spices, gum mastic, rhubarb, cinnamon, aloe wood, and "a thousand other things of value." Above all, the lands have incredible amounts of gold, or thus asserts Columbus, "their Highnesses can see that I shall give them as much gold as they want . . ." [225/14]. Gold abounds everywhere in the possessed islands, according, at least, to the alchemist's eyes of Columbus.

Gold in this epistle is a symbol of material wealth. It would soon acquire, in other of Columbus's texts, spiritual and transcendent value. American gold becomes, in his last writings, the means to wage the final and decisive crusade to repossess the Holy Land, which would be victorious if he, the divinely elected *Christopherens*, leads it. In his feverish 1503 letter from Jamaica, after reiterating to the Crown that he has discovered King Solomon's mines—the legendary, biblical, most abundant gold mines—he even confers redeeming efficacy to gold: "Gold is most excellent . . . it is even able to put souls into heaven."[64]

Natural splendor and gold do not exhaust the riches of this earthly paradise found and possessed by Columbus. There is something else of great value: "people without number" [219/7]. His observations about the people are scant but significant. They comprise four basic points: nakedness ("all go naked, men and women, as their mothers bore them"),[65] military weakness ("they have no iron or steel or weapons"), docility ("show as much love

---

64. *Textos y documentos completos*, 497.

65. Columbus's observation about the nakedness of the Caribbean natives raised an interesting initial theological question: is their nakedness representation of innocence or of savagery? The enigma is slightly suggested in Pope Alexander's 1493 *Inter caetera* bull that mentions both the nakedness and the vegetarian diet of the natives. This is an implicit allusion to Adam and Eve before original sin. When the Spaniards discovered that the natives were willing and able to fight and kill for their lands and freedom, the theological controversy ceased: nakedness became a sign of savagery. Queen Isabella ordered that they be clothed and prohibited their daily baths in the rivers.

as if they were giving their hearts"), and a favorable disposition towards the Christian faith ("their conversion to our holy faith, towards which they are much inclined") [221–223/9–11]. There are other inhabitants of the islands that he had not had time to visit but of whose existence he is certain: people born with tails, hairless people, amazons, and cannibals [223–225/11–14]. Thus are born Western ethnography and anthropology, cradled by the most exotic archaic mythology![66] The cannibals and amazons will entertain from then on the European imagination as objects of fascination and fear.

Right in the middle of the paragraph in which Columbus summarizes the riches of the Caribbean islands, comes the first and fateful suggestion to enslave American natives: "their Highnesses can see that I shall give them as much gold as they want . . . and slaves, as many as they shall order . . ." [225/14]. To Columbus belongs the doubtful honor of the first proposal to enslave New World natives, the first military campaign to enact that enslaving intention, and their first trans-Atlantic shipment as slaves.[67] He is not well versed in juridical and theological niceties, but he knows that the suggestion to enslave indigenous populations has to be conceptually validated. Who are to be enslaved? The answer is laden with theological density: "idolaters" [225/14].

Idolatry, uttered in this epistle for the first time regarding the American natives, will have a long history. Columbus invoked idolatry as a justification to begin the American slave trade, Hernán Cortés to legitimate the conquest of Mexico,[68] and the secular and ecclesiastical authorities in the Andes to expunge aggressively indigenous religiosity.[69] The condemnation of idolatry, spiced with biblical quotations and theological references, becomes the benchmark for the christianization, the enslaving, and the annihilation of many native communities. Idolatry is the theological banner

---

66. Arens, *Man-eating Myth*.

67. Sued Badillo, "Christopher Columbus and the Enslavement of Amerindians in the Caribbean," 71–102.

68. Cortés's Tlaxcala military ordinances invoke idolatry as the main cause for the war against the Aztec kingdom: "In as much . . . the natives of these regions have a culture and veneration of idols, which is a great disservice to God Our Lord, and the devil blinds and deceives them . . . Let us go to uproot the natives of these regions from those idolatries . . . so that they will come to the knowledge of God and of His Holy Catholic faith . . . I affirm that my principal motive in undertaking this war . . . is to bring the natives to the knowledge of our Holy Catholic faith." Cortés, *Documentos cortesianos*, 165.

69. Duviols, *La lutte contre les religions autochtones dans le Pérou colonial*.

to purify theologically the cruelties of war, slavery, and destruction of native religiosity.

The epistle ends in a paean of Christian exaltation. "All Christendom ought to feel joyful and make celebrations and give solemn thanks to the Holy Trinity with many solemn prayers for the turning of so many peoples to our holy faith." But the last word belongs to the promising economic gains: "and afterwards for material benefits, since not only Spain but all Christians will hence have refreshment and profit" [226/15].

Paradise, in Columbus's epistolary fiction, has been found and possessed, in the name of the European Christian God. But, Paradise will soon be lost. Gold will be hard to find and extract. The docile natives will fight and die for their lands and liberty. Between 1494 and 1506, Columbus's fate will be a pilgrimage of bitterness and tribulations, almost as tragic and deadly as that of the native communities whose existence he had inscribed in European literary history.

Paradise had been found, possessed, and, finally, lost. The Argentinian writer Abel Posse aptly concludes his fascinating novel, *Los perros del paraíso* (*The Dogs of Paradise*), with Christopher Columbus, in his native language, sadly whispering: "*Purtroppo c'era il Paradiso . . . !*" ("Unfortunately, it was Paradise").[70] Modern European colonialism had just initiated. It claimed religious roots and sacred legitimations. It began in the name of the Christian Trinity and the crucified Christ. Right here, in the Caribbean, where this Bishops Academy of the Evangelical Lutheran Church of America takes place.

Religion, politics, and empire: their promiscuous miscegenation possesses a long heritage. Resistance to it also . . . . The question stands: Are the Lutheran Bishops from the most powerful nation of the world willing to listen and engage the voices coming from the margins?

---

70. Posse, *Los perros del paraíso*, 223.

4

God the Liberator

Theology, History, and Politics[1]

The Bible is . . . an incendiary device: who knows what we'd make of it, if we ever got our hands on it?

—Margaret Atwood[2]

A THEOLOGICAL *ENFANT TERRIBLE*

Liberation theology was the unforeseen *enfant terrible* in the academic and ecclesial realms of theological production during the last decades of the twentieth century. It brought to the conversation not only a new theme—liberation—but also a new perspective on doing theology and a novel way of referring to God's being and action in history. Its project to reconfigure the interplay between religious studies, history, and politics became a meaningful topic of analysis and dialogue in the general theological discourse. Many scholars perceive in its emergence a drastic epistemological rupture,

---

1. Second lecture delivered to the Evangelical Lutheran Church in America's Bishops Academy, January 4, 2013, in San Juan, Puerto Rico.
2. *Handmaid's Tale*, 103.

a radical change in paradigm, a significant shift in both the ecclesial and social role of theology.

Its origins are diverse, and not only native to theological and ecclesiastical horizons. One important source, neglected by some clerical accounts, was the complex constellation of liberation struggles during the sixties and early seventies. It was a time of social turmoil, when many things seemed out of joint: a strong anti-war protest movement, mainly directed against American military intervention in Vietnam and the global nuclear threat, a spread of decolonization movements all over the Third World, the feminist struggle against masculine patriarchy, a robust challenge to racial bigotry, the Stonewall rebellion (June/69) against homophobia and gay discrimination, student protests in Paris, Prague, Mexico, and New York in opposition to repressive states of all stripes, guerilla insurgencies and social unrest in many Third World nations. Many of these agents of social protest adopted the title of "liberation movement" as their public card of presentation. "Fronts of national liberation" flourished all over Latin America, Africa, and Asia.[3]

Another significant factor was the development of a non-dogmatic Marxism that read Marx's texts as an ethical critique on human oppression and as a projection of a utopian non-oppressive future, sort of a kingdom of freedom. This heterodox way of reading Marx, by authors like the German philosopher Ernst Bloch, made possible something up to then considered unthinkable, a constructive and affirmative dialogue between theology and Marxism at the margins of church and party hierarchies' rigid orthodoxies. Influential in this intellectual milieu was Bloch's 1968 *Atheismus im Christentum,* whose hermeneutical performance diagnoses inside the biblical texts a struggle between the voices of the oppressors and those of the oppressed and provocatively asserts that whoever wants to be a good Marxist should constantly read the Bible (and vice versa, whoever wants to be a good Christian should have Marx as bedside reading).

---

3. The most famous of them, and a model for many, were the Algerian Front of National Liberation, established in 1954, which led the revolt against French colonial domination (brilliantly depicted in Gillo Pontocorvo's 1966 film *Battle of Algiers*), the National Liberation Front for South Vietnam, created in December of 1960, which successfully fought against the division of Viet Nam and the military invasion of the United States, and the Palestine Liberation Organization, founded in 1964 to organize the struggle for Palestinian statehood. See Horne, *Savage War of Peace: Algeria 1954–1962*; Fitzgerald, *Fire in the Lake*, chapter 4: "The National Liberation Front"; and Cobban, *Palestinian Liberation Organisation.*

God the Liberator

Other iconoclast authors like Herbert Marcuse and Franz Fanon were passionately read from Buenos Aires to Berlin, from Berkeley to Nairobi, with intentionalities not limited to the academia.[4] Exiled from Brazil, Paulo Freire delivered scathing critiques of traditional educational systems and promoted a pedagogy for the liberation of the oppressed.[5] Martin Luther King Jr. and Ernesto "Che" Guevara are probably the main emblematic icons and martyrs of those turbulent times. Paul Éluard's poem *Liberté*, recited and sung in many languages, became its poetic hymn.

Within the churches important processes were taking place. Pope John XIII summoned, to the surprise of many, the Second Vatican Council. Progressive Roman Catholic theologians consider Vatican II an important turning point in the modern history of their church.[6] According to their interpretation, the council had three main objectives:

1. To change the attitude of the Roman Catholic Church towards the modern post-Enlightenment intellectual world, from censure and condemnation to openness and dialogue. The Italian word *aggiornamento* became the watchword of the attempts to update the church.

2. To heal the fragmentation of Christianity by inserting the Roman Catholic Church into the emerging ecumenical movement. Delegates from Protestant and Orthodox churches were invited to observe the proceedings of the council. A series of bilateral and multilateral dialogues began between Rome and other Christian denominations.

3. To face with honesty and compassion the plight of a world suffering violence, oppression, and injustice. The council took place in a world sundered by national liberation struggles, civil wars and the painful gap between the haves and the have-nots of the globe. The quest for peace and justice was conceived as an essential dimension of the being in the world of the church.

John XXIII's 1963 encyclical *Pacem in terris*, published in the context of that conciliar process, seemed to be another sign of renewal, from an attitude of anathema to a spirit of dialogue and solidarity. This ecclesiastical openness was accompanied by several theological projects that seemed to shape an alternative way to look at social conflicts.[7] An attempt was made

4. Marcuse, *Essay on Liberation*; Fanon, *Wretched of the Earth*.
5. Freire, *Educação como prática da liberdade*; Freire, *Pedagogía del oprimido*.
6. See Flannery, *Vatican Council II*.
7. Moltmann, *Theologie der Hoffnung*; Metz, *Zur Theologie der Welt*.

to configure a "political theology," as a way to design a creative dialogue with Marxism and post-Enlightenment secular ideologies.[8]

LATIN AMERICAN LIBERATION THEOLOGY

Vatican II was followed by regional synods of bishops. The most famous of them was the general meeting of Latin American Roman Catholic bishops that took place August 26 to September 6, 1968, at Medellín, Colombia. To the amazement of many observers, the Roman Catholic Church, which the radical intelligentsia in the continent had considered the ideological bulwark of prevailing social inequities, was promulgating, as a decisive pastoral challenge, solidarity with the poor and destitute.

If Vatican II opened the theological dialogue with modern rationality, Medellín was perceived as a prophetic convocation against poverty, inequality, and oppression. If Vatican II was mainly concerned with the gap between the church and secular modernity, Medellín, according to this reading, was more concerned with the scandal of social injustice in a Christian continent. In a crucial section of their final resolutions, the Latin American bishops linked the Christian faith with historical and social liberation.

> The Latin American bishops cannot remain indifferent in the face of the tremendous social injustices existent in Latin America, which keeps the majority of our peoples in dismal poverty that in many cases becomes inhuman wretchedness. A deafening cry pours from the throats of millions of men and women asking their pastors for a liberation that reaches them from nowhere...
> Christ, our savior, not only loved the poor... but also centered his mission in announcing liberation to the poor...[9]

Certainly, the Medellín conference was a meeting of bishops, not of theologians. But several Roman Catholic theologians perceived the final documents and the general tone prevailing in the conference as allowing the possibility of rethinking the theological enterprise from the perspective of the poor and downtrodden.[10] Prior to the Medellín meeting, on July 1968, Gustavo Gutiérrez had given a lecture at Chimbote, Perú, significantly

---

8. See Sölle, *Politische Theologie*.
9. Hennelly, *Liberation Theology*, 114, 116, English translation somewhat amended.
10. See Gutiérrez, "Meaning and Scope of Medellín," 59–101.

titled "Toward a Theology of Liberation,"[11] which coupled closely spiritual salvation and human liberation. It proved to be a pioneer text for Latin American liberation theology. It also inaugurated Gutiérrez's more than five decades of fertile theological production.

In 1971 was published the first edition of his most famous book, *Theology of Liberation*, a landmark in Latin American theological writing. His triadic understanding of human liberation—liberation from social and economic oppression, history as a process of self-determined humanization, and redemption from sinfulness—became classic.[12] That same year was also published Hugo Assmann's book *Opresión—Liberación: Desafío a los cristianos*. Assmann placed the emerging liberation theology in the wider context of the Third World: "The contextual starting point of a 'theology of liberation' is the historical situation of domination experienced by the peoples of the Third World."[13] Gutiérrez and Assmann were followed by a spate of other theologians (Leonardo Boff, José Porfirio Miranda, Juan Luis Segundo, Jon Sobrino, Jorge Pixley, among others) whose writings were conceived as expressions of a new intellectual understanding of the faith: liberation theology.[14]

Among the many texts that rocked the placid realm of theological production during those early years of Latin American liberation theology were José Porfirio Miranda's *Marx y la Biblia*, an important contribution to a liberationist hermeneutics, sort of a theological companion to Bloch's *Atheismus im Christentum*, and Juan Luis Segundo's *Liberación de la teología*, with its frontal challenge to traditional scholastic ways of doing theology.

What could be considered to be the main tenets of this theological movement?

1. The retrieval of the subversive memories inscribed in the sacred scriptures, hidden below layers of cultic regulations and doctrinal orthodoxies, but never totally effaced. A specific hermeneutical and

11. It is translated and reproduced in Hennelly, *Liberation Theology*, 62–76.
12. Gutiérrez, *Teología de la liberación*, 67–69.
13. Assmann, *Opresión—Liberación*, 50.
14. See the important book on the origins of Latin American liberation theology by Samuel Silva Gotay, *El pensamiento cristiano revolucionario en América Latina y El Caribe: Implicaciones de la teología de la liberación para la sociología de la religión*, translated into Portuguese as *O pensamento cristão revolucionário na América Latina e no Caribe (1960–1973)*, and into German as *Christentum und Revolution in Lateinamerika und der Karibik: Die Bedeutung der Theologie der Befreiung für eine Soziologie der Religion*.

exegetical concentration in the Exodus story as a paradigm of the liberating character of God's actions,[15] in the prophetic denunciations of injustice and oppression,[16] and in the confrontations of the historical Jesus against the Judean religious authorities and Roman political powers and his solidarity with the nobodies of Judea and Galilee.[17]

2. A historical understanding of Jesus's proclamation of God's kingdom. The kingdom is conceived as referring not to some otherworldly postmortem realm, but to the unceasing hope of a social configuration characterized by justice, solidarity, and freedom. Leonardo Boff and Jon Sobrino perceive Jesus as the Liberator, going back to the semantic roots of the term redemption (the deliverance of a captive or slave).[18]

3. The divine preferential option for the poor, the excluded, and the destitute of this world. The church has to become the church of the poor, sharing their sorrows, hopes and struggles. Initially the accent was mainly socioeconomic, but it was gradually widened to include other categories of social exclusion (indigenous communities, racial and ethnic minorities, women).[19]

4. Theology cannot be reduced to an intellectual understanding of the faith, but must also be a practical commitment for historical transformation. The category of praxis, partly borrowed from Paulo Freire's pedagogy of liberation, partly an adaptation of Marx's eleventh thesis on Feuerbach ("philosophers have hitherto only interpreted the world in various ways; the point is to change it"), acquired normative status. History, therefore, as the realm of the perennial struggle against oppressions and exclusions, emerged as the locus for Christian praxis.[20]

5. God is reconceived not as an immutable and impassible entelechy but, according to the biblical narratives, as a compassionate Eternal Spirit that hears and pays close attention to the cry of the oppressed and whose action in human history has the redemption of the downtrodden and excluded as its ultimate telos. Herein might be located

---

15. Croatto, *Exodus, a Hermeneutics of Freedom*; Pixley, *Exodo, una lectura evangélica*.
16. Houston, *Contending for Justice*.
17. Sobrino, *La fe en Jesucristo*.
18. Boff, *Jesus Cristo libertador; ensaio de cristologia crítica para o nosso tempo*; Sobrino, *Jesucristo liberador*.
19. Boff, *Igreja, carisma e poder*.
20. Pixley and Bastian, *Praxis cristiana y producción teológica*.

liberation theology's main theoretical, epistemological rupture and reconfiguration:[21] a novel way of thinking about God's being and action in history. Instead of contriving arcane scholastic definitions of divine essence, God is referred to as Liberator.

Latin American liberation theology strove to forge a new kind of being the church in the world: the base ecclesial communities as seeds for reconfiguring the church as "the people of God." These congregations were considered expressions of the church's solidarity with the poor and oppressed in their aspirations for liberation and human promotion. An impressive wealth of liturgical, musical, exegetical, homiletical, ethical, and literary resources was produced to promote social and human emancipation. Historical transformation was their key theme. Leonardo Boff even advocated a new genesis of the church.[22]

However, many in the hierarchical church, including some members of the Roman curia apex, viewed with marked distrust their potential disruptions of episcopal authority and moved to restrict their autonomy. Rome was also concerned about the consequences for dogmatic orthodoxy of this new theological perspective. A protracted confrontation ensued that still goes on.

Political power matters. Since their colonial inception, an official linkage between the state and the Roman Catholic Church characterized Latin American nations. The royal patronage exercised by the Iberian crown entailed the acknowledgment by the church of the sovereignty and authority of the metropolitan state, but also the state's recognition of the Roman Catholic Church's primacy in religious affairs. It was sometimes the source of acute conflicts, whenever the ethical conscience of bishops, priests, missionaries, and theologians clashed with the severe exploitation of the native communities. Bartolomé de las Casas, to whose historical significance Gustavo Gutiérrez devoted a magnificent book,[23] is the most famous protagonist of such conflicts. Yet it was a convenient arrangement for both partners, for it conferred a sacred aura to the metropolitan sovereignty and conversely provided the church with state protection. The governments of the new states that emerged after the nineteenth century wars of independence promptly recognized the advantages of the royal patronage and tried to preserve it. This heritage forged a particular brand of Latin American

21. Pimentel Chacón, *Modelos de Dios en las teologías latinoamericanas*.
22. See Boff, *Eclesiogênese*.
23. Gutiérrez, *Las Casas*.

Christendom closely linking the state and the Roman Catholic Church, a condition juridically inscribed in several national constitutions and Vatican concordats.

This official connection between church and state was venerable but also vulnerable. The prophetic and evangelical subversive memories inscribed in the Christian scriptures and traditions surfaced powerfully during the somber and violent times of Latin American military dictatorships (1964–1989) to shake the alliance between the political powers and church authorities. The most famous of the ensuing conflicts took place in the midst of the violent civil war in El Salvador, a place where nuns, priests, lay workers, and even the Primate of the Roman Catholic Church, Archbishop Oscar Arnulfo Romero, were assassinated by the military or their right-wing allies.

Archbishop Romero tried to steer his church to become a defender of the poor and the persecuted. He recognized that the forbearance of the ruling clans was as limited as their economic interests were great. Two weeks before his assassination, in an interview with a Mexican newspaper, he foreshadowed his death and gave a theological and pastoral interpretation of his personal destiny.

> I have frequently been threatened with death... If God accepts the sacrifice of my life, then may my blood be the seed of liberty, and a sign of the hope that will soon become a reality... May my death, if it is accepted by God, be for the liberation of my people, and as a witness of hope in what is to come.[24]

His assassination convinced many church authorities that liberation theology was seriously risking the social wellbeing of the Roman Catholic Church and that a convenient long-standing church-state covenant was endangered by the radical political interventions of some members of the clergy. And they moved decisively to suppress it.

Ecclesiastical and social political considerations were not the only issues of concern for Vatican authorities. Doctrinal orthodoxy matters for the Roman Catholic Church. Under the prefecture of Cardinal Joseph Ratzinger, the Sacred Congregation for the Doctrine of the Faith strongly criticized what it considered liberation theology's ominous doctrinal deviations. On August 6, 1984, it issued, with the approval of Pope John Paul II, the admonishing "Instruction on Certain Aspects of the 'Theology of

---

24. Romero, *Voice of the Voiceless*, 50–51.

Liberation,'" followed by an admonition to Leonardo Boff, and another general critique, "Instruction on Christian Freedom and Liberation" (March 22, 1986). Liberation theology was indicted for borrowing improperly from Marxist thought, emphasizing historical and social liberation to the detriment of spiritual salvation, promoting class struggle instead of reconciliation, disdaining the church's social doctrine, and politicizing biblical hermeneutics, Christology, and the church. The goal of the authoritative reprimands was

> to draw attention . . . to the deviations and risks of deviation, damaging to the faith and to Christian living, that are brought by certain forms of liberation theology. . . the 'theologies of liberation' tend to misunderstand or to eliminate. . . the transcendence and gratuity of liberation in Jesus Christ, true God and true man. . . One needs to be on guard against the politicization of existence, which, misunderstanding the entire meaning of the kingdom of God and the transcendence of the person, begins to sacralize politics and betray the religion of the people in favor of the projects of revolution.[25]

Traditionally indictments like these were able to silence the accused theologians. Not this time. Prompt reactions by Gustavo Gutiérrez, Leonardo Boff, and Juan Luis Segundo were evident signs that Rome had lost the capability to repress the new theological movement.[26] A letter sent by John Paul II to the Brazilian bishops, dated April 9, 1986,[27] has been understood by several scholars as a truce of the growing dispute to avoid a sharp rupture in the Latin American church but also as a validation of the concept of social and political liberation as an important dimension of the church's pastoral mission. Several Roman Catholic theologians have sustained an effort to convince Rome that liberation theology is a valid and legitimate rethinking of the apostolic tradition that does not constitute a threat to the church's orthodoxy or integrity.[28] However, some influential sectors of the Roman curia still look askance at liberation theology as evidenced by the Sacred Congregation for the Doctrine of the Faith's scathing critique of Jon

---

25. Reproduced in Hennelly, *Liberation Theology*, 394, 411–12.

26. See Juan Luis Segundo's strong critical response in his *Teología de la liberación*.

27. Reproduced in Hennelly, *Liberation Theology*, 498–506.

28. See Ellacuría and Sobrino, *Mysterium liberationis*. On November 16, 1989, Ellacuría, then rector of El Salvador's Central American University, five other Jesuits priests, and two domestic servants were assassinated by a group of soldiers.

Sobrino's Christology ("Notification on the works of Father Jon Sobrino, SJ," 11/26/2006).²⁹

Many Roman Catholic narratives disregard other sources that contributed to the birth of liberation theology. In the sixties, several Latin American Protestant churches were undergoing similar processes of rethinking the relationship between salvation, history as the sphere of divine-human encounter, and liberation.³⁰ In fact, the first extensive monograph that focused on historical and social liberation as the central hermeneutical key to conceptualize the Christian faith was the doctoral dissertation of Rubem Alves, a Brazilian Presbyterian. In May of 1968, Alves defended successfully his dissertation at Princeton Theological Seminary. Its title was *Towards a theology of human liberation*.³¹ Alves wrote it under the direction of Richard Shaull, who for a good number of years had been working in theological education in Latin America, first in Colombia and later in Brazil, and who was crucial for the development of a liberationist theology in Protestant Latin American circles.³² Shaull had also been instrumental in the 1970 English publication of Paulo Freire's *Pedagogy of the Oppressed*, a key text in the development of Latin American liberation theology.

Alves's dissertation is a powerful text, written in a splendid literary style. It was published as a book in 1969, two years before Gutiérrez's, but with a significant change in the title: *A Theology of Human Hope*. Apparently, the publishers believed that the concept of "hope," with its obvious connotations to the writings of Jürgen Moltmann, would be more commercially attractive or relevant than "liberation." Yet, despite the change of title, Alves conceptualizes the temporal dialectics proper to theological language in terms of a historical politics of liberation.

> The acts of remembering and hoping that determine the language of the community of faith, therefore, do not have any reality in themselves but in the engagement in the ongoing politics

---

29. See the defense of Sobrino by several dozens of theologians in Vigil, *Bajar de la Cruz a los Pobres*.

30. See Neely, "Protestant Antecedents of the Latin American Theology of Liberation."

31. Alves, "Towards a Theology of Liberation."

32. Shaull, *Hombre, ideología y revolución en América Latina*. See Neely, "Protestant Antecedents," 253: "It is doubtful if any theologian has more consistently and directly contributed to the shaping of the contemporary Protestant theologians of liberation than Richard Shaull."

of liberation which is the situation and condition of theological intelligibility...³³

BLACK LIBERATION THEOLOGY

But as it is wrong to locate the birth of liberation theology exclusively in Roman Catholic circles, it is also mistaken to situate it solely in Latin America. During the times of slavery and racial discrimination in the United States, black churches were communities of solidarity and hope for the enslaved peoples of African ancestry. Then and there the exodus story, the prophetic denunciations, and the story of the crucified but resurrected Jesus became the sung, preached, and hoped for sustaining bases for the narratives of the suffering black communities. Their bodies might be in bondage to their white masters, but their hearts and minds were nourished and comforted by the biblical stories of retribution and redemption.³⁴

In continuity with that history, the African American churches became important protagonists in the civil rights movement for the elimination of racial discrimination. All over the North American South, black preachers became leaders in spreading the challenging message and Gospel music acquired a more historically relevant twist. The speeches of Martin Luther King Jr. are saturated with the cadences, intonations, and biblical images typical of African American preaching.³⁵ The lyrics of "We Shall Overcome," the emblematic hymn of the civil rights movement, is a variant of a prior hymn, "I'll Overcome Some Day," written in 1901 by Charles Albert Tindley, one of the founding fathers of African American Gospel music, and its melody is based upon an even earlier defiant black song, the nineteenth-century spiritual "No more auction block for me," a subversive hymn revived in the twentieth century first by the powerful voice of Paul Robeson and later on by Bob Dylan.

> No more auction block for me
> No more, no more
> No more auction block for me
> Many thousands gone

---

33. Alves, *Theology of Human Hope*, 163. On the theological trajectory of Alves, see Cervantes-Ortiz, *Serie de sueños*.

34. See Raboteau, *Slave Religion* and *A Fire in the Bones*.

35. Carson and Shepard, *Call to Conscience*.

> No more driver's lash for me
> No more, no more
> No more driver's lash for me
> Many thousands gone
>
> No more whip lash for me
> No more, no more
> No more pint of salt for me
> Many thousands gone

In this social and ecclesiastical environment, some African American theologians began to rethink their intellectual role in the epic struggle of their people. Black liberation theology, rooted in the historical experience of slavery and racism, became an important partner in the theological table of dialogue, bringing to the conversation the issues of racial and ethnic discrimination. The foremost of the African American liberation theologians, though certainly not the only one, has been James Cone. In his 1969 book, *Black Theology & Black Power*, he still tentatively wrote: "the work of Christ is essentially a liberating work, directed toward and by the oppressed."[36] It was the foretaste of his 1970 groundbreaking text *A Black Theology of Liberation*. Cone was not one to mince words in his radical transformation of theology.

> It is my contention that Christianity is essentially a religion of liberation. The function of theology is that of analyzing the meaning of that liberation for the oppressed so that they can know that their struggle for political, social, and economic justice is consistent with the gospel of Jesus Christ. Any theology that is indifferent to the theme of liberation is not Christian.
>
> In view of the biblical emphasis on liberation, it seems not only appropriate but necessary to define the Christian community as the community of the oppressed which joins Jesus Christ in his fight for the liberation of humankind.[37]

Black theology of liberation has become an important partner of theological discourse in the academic, ecclesiastical and public social realms in all places where the peoples of African descent have been subjected to

---

36. Cone, *Black Theology & Black Power*, 42.
37. Cone, *Black Theology of Liberation*, v, 3.

FEMINIST LIBERATION THEOLOGY

Simultaneously as Latin American and African American theologians, feminist theologians were questioning radically the patriarchal and misogynistic traditions for so long prevailing in the history of Christianity. Certainly not all theologians would berate women as bitterly as Tertullian did in his treatise *On the Apparel of Women* ["And do you not know that you are (each) an Eve? The sentence of God on this sex of yours lives in this age: the guilt must of necessity live too. You are the devil's gateway: you are the unsealer of that (forbidden) tree: you are the first deserter of the divine law: you are she who persuaded him whom the devil was not valiant enough to attack. You destroyed so easily God's image, man. On account of your desert—that is, death—even the Son of God had to die"],[40] but it is hard to deny the historical importance of the Christian scriptures and traditions as ideological strongholds of patriarchy and female subordination. Key biblical texts, like Genesis 3:16 ("To the woman [God] said: 'your husband shall rule over you'") and 1 Timothy 2:11–14 ("Let a woman learn in silence with full submission. I permit no woman to teach or to have authority over a man; she is to keep silent. For Adam was formed first, then Eve; and Adam was not deceived, but the woman was deceived and became a transgressor") have been constantly read theologically as implying a male priority in the order of creation and a female priority in the disorder of sin and philosophically as conveying an ontological masculine primacy.

Debates in most churches on the possibility of ordaining women led a good number of female theologians to question this misogynic tradition. Texts like Letty Russell's *Human Liberation in a Feminist Perspective: A Theology* (1974), Elisabeth Schüssler Fiorenza's "Feminist Theology as a Critical Theology of Liberation" (1975), and Phillys Trible's *God and the Rhetoric of Sexuality* (1978), among many others, were bellwethers of a feminist liberation theology. Elisabeth Schüssler Fiorenza, in a highly critical and influential book—*In Memory of Her* (1983)—launched a comprehensive

---

38. Including the Caribbean, with its long and dense tradition of Black slavery. See Erskine, *Decolonizing Theology*.

39. See Cone, *Spirituals and Blues*.

40. Tertullian, *On the Apparel of Women*, book I, chapter I, introduction, 14.

theological and hermeneutical challenge to the system of patriarchal dominion for which she coined the term *kyriarchy*. She defines feminist theology as a "critical theology of liberation" that "seeks to develop. . . a historical-biblical hermeneutics of liberation."[41] Her ambitious project is to design a feminist way of looking at biblical and Early Christianity texts with the purpose of retrieving the silenced and repressed memory of the struggle between the early Christian practice of equality in discipleship and the Roman-Hellenistic cultural ethos of benevolent patriarchal dominion.

The targets of severe critique by feminist liberation theology, according to Schüssler Fiorenza, are not only the patriarchal ecclesiastical institutions and theological traditions, but also the premises of masculine hegemony inscribed in the biblical texts themselves. The Bible is thus seen as a site of confrontation and contention between the egalitarian ethos of the early Jesus movement and the patriarchy of later New Testament texts. A feminist theology requires thus a hermeneutics of suspicion and imagination to unearth the polemics hidden in the sacred scriptures. The category of the "poor," foregrounded by the early Latin American theology, is not adequate to describe the inclusive character of the Jesus movement. To it must be added that of "the marginal" or "outcast," as a link between the "church of the poor" and the "church of women." The fundamental hermeneutical norm is therefore not the isolated sacred text but the history of women's struggle for liberation.[42]

However, women of color immediately raised the objection that sex and gender should not be analyzed apart from issues of racial, ethnic, and cultural differences and discriminations. In the kaleidoscopic fragmentation of the human self and subjectivity typical of our postmodernist epoch, feminist liberation theology has engendered a black feminist theology, usually named womanist theology (Karen Baker-Fletcher, Katie Cannon, Emilie Townes, Renita Weems, Traci West, Delores Williams, among others), a Latin American feminist theology (Elsa Tamez, Ivone Gebara, Maria Clara Bingemer, among others), a Latina/Hispanic feminist theology (Ada María Isasi-Díaz, María Pilar Aquino, Michelle González, Daisy Machado, among others), and an Asian-American feminist theology (Kwok Pui-Lan, Namsoon Kang, Wonhee Anne Joh, among others). Rooted in their own history of sorrows, struggles, and hopes these various feminist theologies

---

41. Schüssler Fiorenza, *In Memory of Her*, 29–30.
42. See Schüssler Fiorenza, *Changing Horizons*.

have disrupted significantly the theological endeavor, traditionally a masculine and androcentric academic realm.

The main point of contention in feminist theology relates to the debunking of the conventional images and concepts of God, traditionally perceived as a patriarchal hypostasis. The feminist dispute about sexist and inclusive language finds its culmination in the attempt to dismantle the androcentric captivity of God and theological discourse. How to retool theological thinking so that God might not be construed as a cosmic paterfamilias is probably the biggest challenge. This might be also the main motif—the search for the female dimensions of God—behind the Latino/Hispanic female theologians marked interest in the narratives and worship of the Virgin of Guadalupe[43] and the biblical Sophia.[44]

A POLYPHONY OF LIBERATION THEOLOGIES

During the last decades, in tandem with the growing polycentric character of Christianity, a spate of liberation theologies have emerged from very diverse contexts: Hispanic/Latino, Native American, Asian, Dalit, African, Minjung, Jewish, Palestinian, gay, lesbian, and queer.[45] If social redistribution was the main emphasis of Latin American liberation theology, the demand for the recognition of disdained identities characterizes recent theological trends. Recognition and identity, not only poverty and redistribution,[46] have become crucial issues of theological dialogue and debate. Personal and communal identities, usually left in the dark by traditional ways of doing theology, are now foregrounded.

Naim Ateek and Mitri Raheb, for example, initiate their texts by telling the readers *who* they are: Palestinian Christians.[47] They are both conscious of the tensions in that process of self-identification: *Christian* Palestinians or *Palestinian* Christians? Palestinian theological hermeneutics is also able to foreground the usually silenced ominous dimension of the Exodus story,

---

43. Rodríguez, *Our Lady of Guadalupe*.

44. Rivera, "God at the Crossroads: A Postcolonial Reading of Sophia," 186–203.

45. *Inter alia*, Segovia, "From 1968, through 2008"; Tinker, *Spirit and Resistance*; Pieris, *An Asian Theology of Liberation*; Clarke, *Dalits and Christianity*; Gichaara, "Issues in African Liberation Theology"; Bock, *Minjung Theology*; Ellis, *Toward a Jewish Theology of Liberation*; Ateek, *Justice and Only Justice*; Stuart, *Gay and Lesbian Theologies*.

46. Fraser and Honneth, *Redistribution or Recognition?*

47. Ateek, *Justice and Only Justice*, 13–17; Raheb, *I Am a Palestinian Christian*, 3–14.

both in its biblical context—the atrocious rules of warfare that prescribed servitude or annihilation for the peoples encountered in Israel's route to the "promised land" (Deuteronomy 20: 10–17)—as in the present historical circumstances wherein the Palestinian people is harshly mistreated by the state of Israel. From the painful memory of the *al-nakba* (the "great catastrophe"), it highlights the biblical themes of displacement, dispersion, and captivity, the crucial historical matrixes of the biblical scriptures, as meaningful loci of theological enunciation and reflection.[48] It also, maybe more emphatically than other liberation theologies, underscores the intertwining of justice and reconciliation, truth-telling and forgiveness, prophetic denunciation and peacemaking annunciation.[49]

Possibly the most exciting, intriguing, and controversial contribution to the spreading rainbow of different liberation theologies are the writings of the late Marcella Althaus-Reid, an Argentinean Protestant theologian teaching and writing in Edinburgh, Scotland. In the heartland of conservative Scottish Calvinism, she transgressed all possible frontiers that have traditionally marked theology as a "decent" and "proper" endeavor. In 2000 she published *Indecent Theology: Theological Perversions in Sex, Gender and Politics*[50] and in 2003 *The Queer God*.[51] *Indecent Theology* claims to free liberation theology from its prudish inhibitions, resituating it in the perspective of oppressed sexualities, of concrete bodies in love at the margins of "decency," of sexual dissidence. *Queer God* attempts something even more daring: to rescue God from the monotonous, mono-loving closet where the deity has been relegated. God is subjugated by its forced enclosure in the restrictive role of patriarchal purveyor of a repressive code of thinking and acting. God, not only destitute human beings, needs to be freed and redeemed. Althaus-Reid conceives queer theology as going even further than gay liberation theologies, for it is grounded upon libertine subversions of both oppressive sexual and political heteronomy. Her queer hermeneutics is a methodology of permutations: a fascinating intertextual reading of the sacred scriptures with transgressive and marginal literature to free biblical exegesis from centuries of patriarchal and homophobic exegeses.

48. See Rivera-Pagán, "Toward an Emancipatory Palestinian Theology," 89–117, 399–408.

49. Ateek, *Justice and Only Justice*, chapter 7 ("A Dream of Peace"), 163–175; Raheb, *I Am a Palestinian Christian*, conclusion ("I Have a Dream"), 112–16. See also Ateek, *Palestinian Christian Cry for Reconciliation*.

50. Althaus-Reid, *Indecent Theology*.

51. Althaus-Reid, *The Queer God*.

A LATINO/HISPANIC CONTRIBUTION

Even in the midst of the new American Empire, within the "entrails of the monster," as José Martí phrased it,[52] recent Latino/Hispanic theological productions bring to the fore a vibrant concept of God as Liberator. Mayra Rivera's *The Touch of Transcendence: A Postcolonial Theology of God* (2007)[53] is a readable and intelligent tome comprising a complex array of topics: a deconstructive analysis of how a number of contemporary theologies construe God's transcendence, being, and actions in history, a critical discussion of the possible relevance to theology of the texts of several cultural studies writers (Emmanuel Levinas, Jacques Derrida, Luce Irigaray) and postcolonial authors (Gayatri Spivak, Homi Bhabha, Walter Mignolo), and an examination of the implications of some strands of liberation theology (Latin American, feminist) for the doctrine of God.

It concludes with a very suggestive and seductive proposal to rethink divine transcendence. "Divine transcendence," according to Rivera, "has acquired the reputation of being a tool of patriarchal and imperial self-legitimation."[54] There has been a multi-secular collusion between dualistic metaphysical views of transcendence with multiple entwined projects designed to control and dominate subaltern communities. The critique of those dualistic views and colonizing projects is followed by a complex and rigorous attempt to elaborate a model of divine "relational transcendence" that allows a conception of God as constantly embracing and touching human and cosmic reality, while providing for an endless process of human liberation and for an ethic of solidarity with those "others" whose singularities (national, ethnic, cultural, racial, gender, sexual orientation) are socially signified as emblems of disdain, marginalization, or exploitation. "We will seek a model of transcendence that is attentive to the concrete sociopolitical significance of otherness . . . Our aim to open ourselves to transcendence in the face of the Other leads us to give special attention to our relationships with those who are marginalized in our communities

---

52. Martí, *Obras escogidas*, Vol. 3, 576: "Viví en el monstruo, y le conozco las entrañas:—y mi honda es la de David" ("I lived inside the monster, I know its entrails—and I have David's sling"). See Martí, *Inside the Monster*.

53. Rivera, *Touch of Transcendence*.

54. Ibid., 1.

or simply excluded from them. . ."[55] The touch of divine transcendence is ethically fulfilled in the embracing touch of the pariahs and untouchables.[56]

This is a coherent and impressive theological venture to overcome the dominant dualistic schemes (transcendence/immanence, spirit/body, sacred/profane) that have served as ideological matrices of human subordination and subjugation. Simultaneously, a manner of God-talk is forged that might be faithful both to the biblical witness about the Creator and Sustainer and to the contemporary challenges for social emancipation.

> This model of relational transcendence refuses the 'hard boundary' between the divine and the created. Instead it affirms that the beginning, sustenance, and transformation of the cosmos are intrinsically divine. . . Intracosmic and intercreaturely transcendence are thus inherently linked; both are theologically grounded in an assertion of the beginning of creation in God. . . We aspire to give and receive that which may open for us new paths for continuous liberation. . .[57]

Rivera is well aware that in these times of ours, when new forms of imperial domination are devised, the cross dialogue between polychromic liberation theologies and postcolonial critical studies acquires theoretical relevance and political urgency.[58] Joerg Rieger has well expressed the challenge that this transdisciplinary exchange poises for the concept of God: "What happens when God-talk is turned loose from the powers that be, when it comes from those who bear the marks of colonialism and neocolonialism in their flesh?"[59] From my Latin American and Caribbean context, however, this requires the overcoming of the narrow historical vista of most postcolonial authors, who tend to focus their critical gaze to post Enlightenment imperial formations.[60] After all, modern Western imperial domi-

---

55. Ibid., 82.

56. Here Rivera quotes one of Althaus-Reid's transgressive texts: "God is to be found in the presence of the untouchables. . . [Transcendence] is God touching its own limits in the untouchables." Althaus-Reid, "El Tocado (Le Toucher)," 394.

57. Rivera, *Touch of Transcendence*, 133, 140.

58. Keller, Nausner, and Rivera, *Postcolonial Theologies*; Kwok, *Postcolonial Imagination and Feminist Theology*; Joh, *Heart of the Cross*; Rivera, *Touch of Transcendence*; Rieger, *Christ & Empire*; Kwok, Compier, and Rieger, *Empire: The Christian Tradition*.

59. Rieger, "Liberating God-Talk," 220.

60. See Fernando Segovia's sharp and critical exposition of the theoretical convergences between postcolonial studies and anti-imperial biblical hermeneutics: "Mapping the Postcolonial Optic in Biblical Criticism," 23–78.

God the Liberator

nation began with the sixteenth century Iberian conquest of the Caribbean archipelago and the Latin American territories.[61]

PROVISIONAL PREDICTIONS

Although several observers have predicted the demise of liberation theology, a better way to describe its actual condition is its proliferation by means of the fragmentation of subversive identities. What is striking is its ability to morph from its antecedents into a plethora of new movements. The original intuition of "preferential option for the poor" has been widened to the "excluded," "marginalized," "victims," "disdained," "downtrodden." There are even signs of a vigorous reawakening of liberation theology, for its main sources are still with us:

1. The worldwide growing social and economic inequities entailed by the global hegemony of a neoliberal capitalist system of free market that validates profit as the hallmark of success. Poverty and injustice still prevail, tragically distorting the fate of millions of human beings all over our planet. Transnational corporations play lucrative chess games with their lives and labors, aborting illusions and shattering dreams.

2. But also everywhere the "wretched of the earth," as Franz Fanon called them, demand a different and alternative social order and forge innovative models of protest and resistance. Their particular struggles might be different but not incompatible or incommensurable. Some resist poverty and economic misery, others demand full recognition for their racial, ethnic, or cultural identity, others assert the integrity and dignity of their gender or sexual orientation. These diverse perspectives complicate but also widen significantly the horizons of today's struggles for liberation.

3. The constant retrieval, by many Christians, of the rebel and subversive memories hidden in the biblical texts and Christian traditions. It is impossible to silence or repress completely the rebellious tones of the Exodus narrative, the denunciatory voice of the prophets, Jesus's disturbing proclamation of good news for the poor and the captives, the attempts by the early Christian movement to shape a participatory

---

61. Dussel, *1492: El encubrimiento del otro*; Mignolo, *Darker Side of the Renaissance*; Rivera-Pagán, "Doing Pastoral Theology in a Post-Colonial Context," 1–28.

and sharing community, or the anti-imperial tone of Revelation. Those memories, which constitute the core of the sacred scriptures, precipitate in the mind and heart of many readers the commitment for liberation. They lead to multiple and diverse meaningful efforts to shape for theology a public emancipatory role.[62]

4. God matters. Even in these postmodernist and cybernetic times people care about God. In the midst of present disturbances and conflicts, the "battle for God," as Karen Armstrong so aptly has named it,[63] rages ferociously. In the fascinating and perplexing kaleidoscope of human social existence, God is reimagined as the ultimate source of hope for the oppressed and downtrodden. When the social miseries that afflict so many communities become unbearable, beyond and besides the tiresome quarrels of religious fundamentalism and dogmatic secularism, the memory of God the Liberator erupts again and again: "When the Egyptians treated us harshly and afflicted us. . . we cried to the Lord, the God of our ancestors; the Lord heard our voice and saw our affliction, our toil, and our oppression. The Lord brought us out of Egypt with a mighty hand and an outstretched arm. . ." (Deuteronomy 26:6–8). As the influential 1985 South African *Kairos* document categorically states: "Throughout the Bible God appears as the liberator of the oppressed."

These are the factors that counter and resist the ruling imperial project of controlling and policing the frontiers of human imagination. Deeply felt fears and hopes, as the astute David Hume noted more than two centuries ago,[64] are able to agitate hearts and spirits and to move minds to think the otherwise unthinkable. Suddenly, at the end of the epoch so aptly named the "Age of Extremes" by Eric Hobsbawm,[65] two tendencies clash: the first announces with glib satisfaction "the end of history," the obliteration of transformative social utopias;[66] the second, from the entrails of the subordinated subjects,[67] proclaims a new insurrection of human hopes for "another possible world."[68]

62. See Valentin, *Mapping Public Theology*.
63. Armstrong, *Battle for God*.
64. Hume, *Natural History of Religion*.
65. Hobsbawm, *Age of Extremes*.
66. Fukuyama, *End of History*.
67. Hinkelammert, *El grito del sujeto*.
68. Pixley et al., *Por un mundo otro*.

The essential imperative might be to remember and radicalize the prophetic words written by the imprisoned Dietrich Bonhöffer, in a note surreptitiously preserved by his friend Eberhard Bethge: "We have for once learnt to see the great events of world history from below, from the perspective of the outcast, the suspects, the maltreated, the powerless, the oppressed, the reviled—in short, from the perspective of those who suffer."[69]

---

69. Bonhöffer, *Letters and Papers from Prison*, 16.

5

Xenophilia or Xenophobia
Towards a Theology of Migration[1]

I have Dutch, nigger, and English in me,
and either I'm nobody, or I'm a nation.
—Derek Walcott[2]

To survive the Borderlands
you must live *sin fronteras*
be a crossroads.
—Gloria Anzaldúa[3]

---

1. Third lecture delivered to the Evangelical Lutheran Church in America's Bishops Academy, January 5, 2013, in San Juan, Puerto Rico.
2. Walcott, "Schooner 'Flight,'" 346.
3. Anzaldúa, *Borderlands/La Frontera*, 217.

A HOMELESS MIGRANT ARAMEAN

The Bible's first confession of faith begins with a story of pilgrimage and migration: "A wandering Aramean was my ancestor; he went down into Egypt and lived there as an alien. . ." (Deut 26:5). We might ask, did that "wandering Aramean" and his children have the proper documents to reside in Egypt? Were they "illegal aliens"? Did he and his children have the proper Egyptian social security credentials? Did they speak properly the Egyptian language?

We know at least that he and his children were strangers in the midst of a powerful empire, and that as such they were both exploited and feared. This is the fate of many immigrants. In their reduced circumstances they are usually compelled to perform the least prestigious and most strenuous kinds of menial work. But at the same time they awaken the schizophrenic paranoia typical of empires, powerful and yet fearful of the stranger, of the "other," especially if that stranger resides within its frontiers and becomes populous. More than half a century ago, Franz Fanon brilliantly described the peculiar gaze of so many white French people at the growing presence of Black Africans and Caribbeans in their national midst.[4] Scorn and fear are entwined in that stare.

The biblical creedal story continues: "When the Egyptians treated us harshly and afflicted us, by imposing hard labor on us, we cried to the . . . God of our ancestors; the Lord heard our voice and saw our affliction . . . and our oppression" (26:6). So important was this story of migration, slavery, and liberation for the biblical people of Israel that it became the core of an annual liturgy of remembrance and gratitude. The already quoted statement of faith was to be solemnly recited every year in the thanksgiving liturgy of the harvest festival. It reenacted the wounded memory of the afflictions and humiliations suffered by an immigrant people, strangers in the midst of an empire; the recollection of their hard and arduous labor, of the contempt and scorn that is so frequently the fate of the foreigner with a different skin pigmentation, language, religion, or culture. But it was also the memory of the events of liberation, when God heard the dolorous cries of the suffering immigrants. And the remembrance of another kind of migration, in search of a land where they might live in freedom, peace, and righteousness, a land they might call theirs.

---

4. Fanon, *Peau Noir, Masques Blancs*.

We might ask: Who today might be the wandering Arameans and what nation might represent Egypt these days, a strong but fearful empire?

DILEMMAS AND CHALLENGES OF MIGRATION

The United States is undergoing a significant increase of its Latino/Hispanic population. In 1975, little more than 11 million Hispanics made up just over 5 percent of the U.S. inhabitants. Today they number approximately nearly 47 million, around 15 percent of the nation, its largest minority group. Recent projections estimate that by 2050 the Latino/Hispanic share of the U.S. population might be between 26 to 32 percent. This demographic growth has become a complex political and social debate for it highlights sensitive and crucial issues, like national identity and compliance with the law. It also threatens to unleash a new phase in the sad and long history of American racism and xenophobia,[5] one that, according to the Sri Lankan novelist Ambalavaner Sivanandan, might be termed "xeno-racism."[6]

Two concerns have become important topics of public discourse:

1. What to do regarding the growth of unauthorized migration? Possibly about a quarter of the Hispanic/Latino adults are unauthorized immigrants. For a society that prides itself on its law and order tradition, that represents a serious breach of its juridical structure.

2. What does this dramatic increase in the Latino/Hispanic population might convey for the cultural and linguistic traditions of the United States, its mores and styles of collective self-identification?

Unfortunately, the conversation about these complex and sensitive issues takes place in an environment clouded by the gradual development of xenophobic attitudes. There are signs of an increasing hostile reaction to what the Mexican-American writer Richard Rodríguez has termed "the browning of America."[7] One can clearly recognize this mind-set in the frequent use of the derogatory term "illegal alien." As if the illegality would define not a specific delinquency, but the entire being of the migrant. We all know the dire and sinister connotations that "alien" has in popular American culture, thanks in part to the sequence of four "Alien" [1979,

---

5. Min, *Encyclopedia of Racism in the United States* (3 vols.). Higham, *Strangers in the Land*.

6. As quoted in Snyder, *Asylum-Seeking, Migration and Church*, 93.

7. Rodríguez, *Brown*.

1986, 1992, and 1997] films with Sigourney Weaver fighting back atrocious creatures.⁸

Let me briefly mention some key elements of this emerging xenophobia:

1. There is what one might call the Lou Dobbs syndrome: The spread of fear regarding the so-called "broken borders," the possible proliferation of Third World epidemic diseases, and the alleged increase of criminal activities by undocumented immigrants.⁹ A shadowy sinister specter is created in the minds of the public: the image of the intruder and threatening "other."

2. The xenophobic stance intensifies the post 9/11 attitudes of fear and phobia regarding the strangers, those people who are here but who do not seem to belong here. Surveillance of immigration is now located under the Department of Homeland Security. This administrative merger links two basically unrelated problems: threat of terrorist activities and unauthorized migration.

3. Though U.S. racism and xenophobia have had traditionally different targets—people with African ancestry the first (be they slaves or free citizens), marked by their dark skin pigmentation, foreign-born immigrants the second, distinguished by their particular language, religiosity, and collective memory—in the case of Latin American immigrants both nefarious prejudices converge and coalesce¹⁰ (as was also the case with the nineteenth century Chinese indentured servants, which led to the infamous 1882 Chinese Exclusion Act).¹¹

4. There has been a significant increase of aggressive anti-immigrant groups. According to a report by the Southern Poverty Law Center, "'nativist extremist groups—organizations that go beyond mere advocacy of restrictive immigration policy to actually confront or harass suspected immigrants—jumped from 173 groups in 2008 to 309 last year [2009]. Virtually all of these vigilante groups have appeared since the spring of 2005."¹²

---

8. See also Patrick J. Buchanan's book, with the inflammatory title, *State of Emergency: The Third World Invasion and Conquest of America.*

9. Leonhardt, "Truth, Fiction and, and Lou Dobbs," C1.

10. Fredrickson, *Diverse Nations.*

11. Miller, *Unwelcome Immigrant.*

12. Potok, "Rage in the Right."

5. Proposals coming from the White House, Congress, states, and counties have tended to be excessively punitive.

   Examples of such punitive measures are:

   a. A projected wall along the Mexican border (compare it to Ephesians 2:14, "Christ . . . has broken down the dividing wall").

   b. The criminalization as felony not only of illegal immigration but also of any action by legal residents that might provide assistance to undocumented immigrants.[13]

   c. Draconian legislation prescribing mandatory detention and deportation of non-citizens, even for alleged minor violations of law. Arizona's notorious and contentious Senate Bill 1070 is a prime example of this infamous trend. It has been followed by Alabama's even harsher anti-immigrants legislation (House Bill 56), soon to be cloned by other states.

   d. Proposed legislation to curtail access to public services (health, education, police protection, legal services, drivers' licenses) by undocumented migrants.

   e. Some prominent right-wing politicians have suggested the possibility of revising the first section of the fourteenth amendment of the US constitution.[14] Their purpose, apparently, is to deprive the children of immigrants of their constitutional right of citizenship. A campaign against the so-called "anchor babies" has been part and parcel of the most strident xenophobic campaign in years.

---

13. This was one of the most controversial sections of the "Border Protection, Antiterrorism, and Illegal Immigration Control Act of 2005" (H.R. 4437), a bill approved by Congress but not by the Senate. Several religious leaders expressed their objection to it. The Los Angeles Roman Catholic cardinal archbishop Roger Mahony, in an article published March 22, 2006 in *The New York Times* under the title "Called by God to Help," asserted that "denying aid to a fellow human being violates a law with a higher authority than Congress — the law of God" and warned that the priests of his diocese might disobey the bill in case it would be finally approved.

14. The first sentence of that section reads as follows: "All persons born or naturalized in the United States, and subject to the jurisdiction thereof, are citizens of the United States and of the State wherein they reside." The second sentence of that same first section has also become center of attention of another key dispute in the U.S.: whether its tenets of "due process of law" and "equal protection of the laws" preclude any legislative prohibition of gay marriage.

Xenophilia or Xenophobia

f. A significant intensification of raids, detentions, and deportations. This is transforming several migrant communities into a clandestine underclass of fear and dissimulation. Some legal scholars have even suggested that the United States is becoming a "deportation nation."[15] It brings to mind the infamous Mexican deportation program, authorized in 1929 by President Herbert Hoover. That program led, according to some scholars, to the forceful deportation of approximately one million people of Mexican descent, many of which were, in fact, American citizens.[16]

g. Congress has been unable to approve the Development, Relief and Education for Alien Minors Act (DREAM Act), that would provide conditional permanent residency to certain deportable foreign-born students who graduate from U.S. high schools, are of good moral character, were brought to the U.S. illegally as minors, and have been in the country continuously for at least five years prior to the bill's enactment, if they complete two years in the military or at an academic institution of higher learning.

The xenophobia and scapegoating of the "stranger in our midst" has resulted in the chaotic condition that now plagues the immigration system in the United States, judicially, politically, and socially. All recent attempts to enact a comprehensive immigration reform have floundered thanks to the resistance of influential sectors that have been able to propagate efficaciously the fear of the "alien."[17] The increasing support that such phobic anxiety against the "outsiders" within the frontiers of the nation seems to enjoy among substantial sectors of the American public brings to mind Alexis de Tocqueville's astute critical observation: "I know no country in which there is so little true independence of mind and freedom of discussion as in America... In America, the majority raises very formidable barriers to the liberty of opinion."[18]

---

15. Kanstroom, *Deportation Nation*.

16. Hoffman, *Unwanted Mexican Americans in the Great Depression*; Balderrama and Rodríguez, *Decade of Betrayal*.

17. Matthew Soerens and Jenny Hwang provide a succinct and precise summary of the most recent failed attempts to enact a comprehensive immigration legislative and juridical reform in their book *Welcoming the Stranger*, 138–58.

18. Tocqueville, *Democracy in America*, 192.

Essays from the Margins

FROM A CLASH OF CIVILIZATIONS TO A CLASH OF CULTURES

In this social context tending towards xenophobia and racism, the late Professor Samuel P. Huntington wrote some important texts about what he perceived as a Hispanic/Latino threat to the cultural and political integrity of the United States. Huntington was chairman of Harvard's Academy for International and Area Studies, and cofounder of the journal *Foreign Policy*. He was also the intellectual father of the theory of the "clash of civilizations,"[19] with disastrous consequences for the foreign policies of the United States.

In 2004, Huntington published an extended article in *Foreign Policy*, titled "The Hispanic Challenge," followed by a lengthy book, *Who Are We? The Challenges to America's National Identity*. The former prophet of an unavoidable civilizational abyss and conflict between the West and the Rest (specially the Islamic nations) became the proclaiming apostle of an emerging nefarious cultural conflict inside the United States. Immersed in a dangerous clash of civilizations *ad extra*, this messenger of doom prognosticated that the United States is also entering into a grievous clash of cultures *ad intra*.

American national identity seems a very complex issue for it deals with an extremely intricate and highly diverse history. But Huntington has, surprisingly, a simple answer: The United States is mainly identified by its "Anglo-Protestant culture" and not only by its liberal republican democratic political creed. It has been, according to this historical reconstruction, a nation of settlers rather than immigrants. The first British pioneers transported not only their bodies, but also their fundamental cultural and religious viewpoints, what Huntington designates as "Anglo-Protestant culture." In the formation of this collective identity, Christian devotion—the Congregational pilgrims, the Protestantism of dissent, the Evangelical Awakenings—has been meaningful and crucial. This national identity has also been forged by a long history of wars against a succession of enemies (from the Native Americans to the Islamic jihadists). There is a certain romantic nostalgia in Huntington's thesis, an emphasis on the foundations of American culture and identity, in their continuities rather than its evolutions and transformations.

---

19. Huntington, "Clash of Civilizations?," 22–49; *Clash of Civilizations and the Remaking of World Order*.

But the main objective of Huntington is to underline the uncertainties of the present trends regarding his nation's collective self-understanding. After the dissolution of the Soviet threat, he perceives a significant neglect of the American national identity. National identity seems to require the image of a dangerous adversary, what he terms the "perfect enemy." The prevailing trend is supposedly one of a notable decline and loss of intensity and salience of U.S. awareness of national identity and loyalty.

But then emerges the sinister challenge of the Latin-American migratory invasion. It is not similar to previous migratory waves. Its contiguity, intensity, lack of education, territorial memory, constant return to the homeland, preservation of language, retention of homeland culture, national allegiance and citizenship, its distance to Anglo-Protestant culture, its alleged absence of a Puritan work ethic, makes it unique and unprecedented. This immigration constitutes, according to Huntington, "a major potential threat to the cultural and possibly political integrity of the United States."[20] This Harvard professor has discovered and named America's newest "perfect enemy" . . . the Latin American migrant!

Huntington's discomfiture is intense regarding the encroachment of Spanish in the American public life. He calls attention to the fact that now in some states more children are ominously christened José rather than Michael. This increasing public bilingualism threatens to fragment the U.S. linguistic integrity. Linguistic bifurcation becomes a veritable menacing Godzilla. He neglects altogether the economic causes for the Latin-American migration—its financial and social benefits both for the sending (remittances)[21] and the receiving nations (lower wages for manual jobs).[22] He does not seem to have any concern regarding the process whereby they become new *douloi* and *μέτοικοι*, helots at the margins of society, in a kind of social Apartheid, cleaning stores, cooking meals, doing dishes, cutting grass, picking tomatoes and oranges, painting buildings, washing cars, staying out of the way . . .

Obfuscated by Huntington are the consequences of the present trend among metropolitan Third World diasporas towards holding dual

20. Huntington, *Who Are We?*, 243.

21. Ratha, "Dollars Without Borders,": "[R]emittances are proving to be one of the more resilient pieces of the global economy in the downturn, and will likely play a large role in the economic development and recovery of many poor countries" (http://www.foreignaffairs.com/articles/65448/dilip-ratha/dollars-without-borders).

22. This is a serious flaw in many ethnocentric critiques of immigration issues according to Blázquez Ruiz, "Derechos humanos, inmigración, integración," 86, 93.

citizenship. An increasing number of Latin-American nations now recognize and promote double citizenship, a process that leads to multiple national and cultural loyalties and to what Huntington classifies, with a disdainful and pejorative tone, "ampersand peoples." Dual citizenship, Huntington rightly recognizes, leads to dual national loyalties and identities. Huntington perceives this trend towards dual citizenship and national belongingness as a violation and disruption of the Oath of Allegiance and the Pledge of Allegiance, essential components of "America's national identity" secular liturgy.

He seems to suggest stricter policies regarding illegal migration, stronger measures to enforce cultural assimilation of the legal immigrants, and the rejection of dual citizenship. This perspective would not only be utterly archaic; it might also become the theoretical underground for a new wave of xenophobic white nativism.[23] The train has already left that outdated station. What is now required is a wider acceptance and enjoyment of multiple identities and loyalties and, if religious compassion truly matters, a deeper concern regarding the burdens and woes of displaced peoples. The time has come to prevail over the phobia of diversity and to learn how to appreciate and enjoy the dignity of difference.[24] For, as Dale Irvin has recently asserted, "the actual world that we are living in... is one of transnational migrations, hyphenated and hybrid identities, cultural conjunctions and disjunctions."[25]

Do the Latinos/Hispanics truly represent "a major potential threat to the cultural and possibly political integrity of the United States," as Huntington has argued? Whether that is something to lament, denounce, or celebrate depends on the eyes of the beholder. Maybe, just maybe, it would not be that negative a historical outcome if Latino immigrants prove in fact to be that dramatic and decisive "major potential threat to the cultural and possibly political integrity of the United States."[26]

---

23. A substantially more nuanced and intellectually complex analysis of the different aspects of immigration in the United States is provided by Portes and Rumbaut, *Immigrant America*.

24. Sacks, *Dignity of Difference*.

25. Irvin, "Church, the Urban and the Global," 181.

26. Yet, at least Huntington recognizes the critical urgency of the substantial Latin-American immigration for the cultural and political integrity of the United States. Cornel West, in another key text published in 2004, *Democracy Matters*, remains cloistered in the traditional White/Black American racial dichotomy and is unable to perceive the salience and perils of xenophobia and nativism as a chauvinistic reply to immigration. Is

XENOPHILIA: TOWARDS A BIBLICAL THEOLOGY OF MIGRATION

Migration and xenophobia are serious social quandaries. But they also convey urgent challenges to the ethical sensitivity of religious people and persons of good will. The first step we need to take is to perceive this issue from the perspective of the immigrants, to pay cordial (that is, deep from our hearts) attention to their stories of suffering, hope, courage, resistance, ingenuity, and, as so frequently happens in the wildernesses of the American Southwest, death.[27] Many of the unauthorized migrants have become *nobodies*, in the apt title of John Bowe's book, *disposable people*, in Kevin Bales' poignant phrase, or, as Zygmunt Bauman poignantly reminds us, *wasted lives*.[28] They are the Empire's new μέτοικοι, *douloi*, modern servants. Their dire existential situation cannot be grasped without taking into consideration the upsurge in global inequalities in these times of unregulated international financial hegemony. For many human beings the excruciating alternative is between misery in their third-world homeland or marginalization in the rich West/North, both fateful destinies intimately linked together.[29]

Will the Latino/Hispanics, during these early decades of the twenty-first century, become the new national scapegoats? Do they truly represent "a major potential threat to the cultural and possibly political integrity of the United States"? This is a vital dilemma that the United States has up to now been unable to face and solve. We are not called, here and now, to solve it. But allow me, from my perspective as a Hispanic and Latin-American

there any possible conceptual manner of bridging the concerns of the African-American ghettoes, struggling against color-coded racism, and the growing Latino/Hispanic barrios, facing an insidious cultural disdain? Both communities suffer from lack of recognition of their genuine human dignity, which should imply more than mere tolerance for their distinctive cultural traits, of socio-economic deprivation and political powerlessness. An always complex and difficult to achieve dialectics between cultural recognition and social-economic redistribution might be the key clue for solving this dilemma. See Fraser and Honneth, *Redistribution or Recognition*. Ernesto Laclau and Chantal Mouffe emphasize this dialectics in the preface to the new edition of their famed text, *Hegemony and Socialist Strategy*, xviii: "One of the central tenets of *Hegemony and Socialist Strategy* is the need to create a chain of equivalence among the various democratic struggles against subordination... to tackle issues of both 'redistribution' and 'recognition.'"

27. See the poignant article by Harding, "Deaths Map," 7–13.
28. Bowe, *Nobodies*; Bales, *Disposable People*; Bauman, *Wasted Lives*.
29. Milanovic, "Global Inequality and the Global Inequality Extraction Ratio: The Story of the Past Two Centuries,"; Stalker, *Workers Without Frontiers*.

Christian theologian, to offer some critical observations that might illuminate our way in this bewildering labyrinth.

We began this essay with the annual creedal and liturgical memory of a time when the people of Israel were aliens in the midst of an empire, a vulnerable community, socially exploited and culturally scorned. It was the worst of times. It became also the best of times: the times of liberation and redemption from servitude. That memory shaped the sensitivity of the Hebrew nation regarding the strangers, the aliens, within Israel. Their vulnerability was a reminder of their own past helplessness as immigrants in Egypt, but also an ethical challenge to care for the foreigners inside Israel.[30]

Caring for the stranger became a key element of the Torah, the covenant of justice and righteousness between Yahweh and Israel. "When an alien resides with you in your land, you shall not oppress the alien. The alien who resides with you shall be to you as the citizen among you; you shall love the alien as yourself, for you were aliens in the land of Egypt: I am the Lord your God" (Leviticus 19:33–34). "You shall not oppress a resident alien; you know the heart of an alien, for you were aliens in the land of Egypt" (Exodus 23:9). "The Lord your God is God of gods . . . who executes justice to the orphan and the widow, and who loves the strangers, providing them food and clothing. You shall also love the stranger, for you were strangers in the land of Egypt" (Deuteronomy 10:17–19). "You shall not withhold the wages of poor and needy laborers, whether other Israelites or aliens who reside in your land in one of your towns . . . You shall not deprive a resident alien . . . Remember that you were a slave in Egypt and the Lord redeemed you from there . . ." (Deuteronomy 24:14, 17–18). The twelve curses that, according to Deuteronomy 27, Moses instructs the Israelites to liturgically proclaim at their entrance to the promised land, include the trilogy of orphans, widows and strangers as privileged recipients of collective solidarity and compassion: "Cursed be anyone who deprives the alien, the orphan, and the widow of justice" (Deuteronomy 27:19).

The prophets constantly chastised the ruling elites of Israel and Judah for their social injustice and their oppression of the vulnerable people. Who were those vulnerable persons? The poor, the widows, the fatherless children, and the foreigners. "The princes of Israel . . . have been bent on shedding blood . . . the alien residing within you suffers extortion; the orphan and the widow are wronged in you" (Ezekiel 22:6–7). After condemning with the harshest words possible the apathy and inertia of temple religiosity

---

30. See Ramírez Kidd, *Alterity and Identity in Israel*.

in Jerusalem, the prophet Jeremiah, in the name of God, commands the alternative: "Thus says the Lord: Act with justice and righteousness . . . And do no wrong or violence to the alien, the orphan, and the widow . . ." (Jeremiah 7:6). He went on to reprove the king of Judah with harsh admonishing words: "Thus says the Lord: Act with justice and righteousness, and deliver from the hand of the oppressor anyone who has been robbed. And do no wrong or violence to the alien, the orphan, and the widow. . . If you do not heed these words, I swear by myself, says the Lord, that this house shall become a desolation" (Jeremiah 22:3, 5). The prophet paid a costly price for those daring admonitions.

The divine command to care for the stranger was the matrix of an ethics of hospitality. As evidence of his righteousness, Job witnesses that "the stranger has not lodged in the street" for he always "opened the doors of my house" to board the foreigner (Job 31:32). It was the violation of the divinely sanctioned code of hospitality that led to the dreadful destruction of Sodom (Genesis 19:1–25).[31] The perennial temptation is xenophobia. The divine command, enshrined in the Torah is xenophilia—the love for those whom we usually find very difficult to love: the strangers, the aliens, the foreign sojourners.

The command to love the sojourners and resident foreigners in the land of Israel emerges from two foundations.[32] One, has already been mentioned—the Israelites had been sojourners and resident foreigners in a land not of their own ("for you were strangers in the land of Egypt") and should, therefore, be sensitive to the complex existential stress of communities living in the midst of a nation whose dominant inhabitants speak a different language, venerate dissimilar deities, share distinct traditions, and commemorate different historical founding events. Love and respect towards the stranger and the foreigner is thus, in these biblical texts, construed as an essential dimension of Israel's national identity. It belongs to the essence and nature of the people of God.

A second source for the command of care towards the immigrant foreigner is that it corresponds to God's way of being and acting in history:

---

31. Sodom's transgression of the hospitality code was part of a culture of corruption and oppression, according to Ezekiel 16:49—"This was the guilt of your sister Sodom: she and her daughters had pride, excess of food, and prosperous ease, but did not aid the poor and needy." The homophobic construal of Sodom's sinfulness, which led to the term sodomy, is a later (mis)interpretation. See Jordan, *The Invention of Sodomy in Christian Theology*.

32. Cervantes Gabarrón, "El inmigrante en las tradiciones bíblicas," 262.

"The Lord watches over the strangers" (Psalm 146:9a),[33] "God... executes justice for the orphan and the widow and loves the strangers..." (Deuteronomy 10:18). God takes sides in history, favoring the most vulnerable: the poor, the widows, the orphans and the strangers. "I will be swift to bear witness... against those who oppress the hired workers in their wages, the widow, and the orphan, against those who thrust aside the alien, and do not fear me, says the Lord of hosts" (Malachi 3:5). Solidarity with the marginalized and excluded corresponds to God's being and acting in history.

How comforting it would be to stop right here, with these fine biblical texts of xenophilia, of love for the stranger. But the Bible happens to be a disconcerting book. It contains a disturbing multiplicity of voices, a perplexing polyphony that frequently complicates our theological hermeneutics. Regarding many key ethical dilemmas, we find in the Bible often times not only different, but also conflicting, even contradictory perspectives. Too frequently we jump from our contemporary labyrinths into a darker and sinister scriptural maze.

In the Hebrew Bible we also discover statements with a distinct and distasteful flavor of nationalist xenophobia. Leviticus 25 is usually read as the classic text for the liberation of the Israelites who have fallen into indebted servitude. Indeed it is, as its famed tenth verse so eloquently manifests: "Proclaim liberty throughout all the land unto all the inhabitants thereof."[34] But it also contains a nefarious distinction: "As for the male and female slaves whom you may have, it is from the nations around you that you may acquire male and female slaves. You may also acquire them from among the aliens residing with you, and from their families... and they may be your property... These you may treat as slaves..." (Leviticus 25:44–46). And what about the terrifying fate imposed upon the foreign wives (and their children), in the epilogues of Ezra and Nehemiah? They are thrown away, expelled, as sources of impurity and contamination of the faith and culture of the people of God.[35] In the process of reconstructing

---

33. This periscope deserves to be quoted in its entirety: "The Lord sets the prisoners free; the Lord opens the eyes of the blind. The Lord lifts up those who are bowed down; the Lord loves the righteous. The Lord watches over the strangers; he upholds the orphan and the widow, but the way of the wicked he brings to ruin" (Psalm 146:8–9).

34. This text is inscribed in Philadelphia's Liberty Bell, a venerated U.S. icon.

35. For a sharp critical analysis of the xenophobic and misogynist theology underlining Ezra and Nehemiah, see Cook Steicke, *La mujer como extranjera en Israel*. Snyder contrasts what she terms "the ecology of fear," exemplified by the banishment of foreign wives (and their children) in Ezra and and Nehemiah, with an "ecology of faith," as

Jerusalem, "Ezra and Nehemiah demonstrate the growing presence of xenophobia," as the Palestinian theologian Naim Ateek has appropriately highlighted. He immediately adds: "Ezra and Nehemiah demonstrate the beginning of the establishment of a religious tradition that leaned toward traditionalism, conservatism, exclusivity, and xenophobia."[36] Let us also not forget the atrocious rules of warfare that prescribes forced servitude or annihilation of the peoples encountered in Israel's route to the "promised land" (Deuteronomy 20:10–17). These all are, in Phyllis Trible's apt expression, "texts of terror."[37]

The problem with some evangelically oriented books like Matthew Soerens & Jenny Hwang's *Welcoming the Stranger* and M. Daniel Carroll R., *Christians at the Border: Immigration, the Church, and the Bible* is that their hermeneutical strategy evades completely and intentionally those biblical texts that might have xenophobic connotations. Both books, for example, narrate the postexilic project of rebuilding Jerusalem, physically, culturally and religiously, under Nehemiah,[38] but silence the expulsion of the foreign wives, an important part of that project (Ezra 9–10, Nehemiah 13:23–31). The rejection of foreign wives in the biblical texts Ezra and Nehemiah does not seem too different from several modern anti-immigrants' xenophobia: those foreign wives have a different linguistic, cultural, and religious legacy—"half of their children . . . could not speak the language of Judah, but spoke the language of various peoples. And I contended with them and cursed them and beat some of them and pulled out their hair" (Nehemiah 13:24–25).

This conundrum is a constant irritating *modus operandi* of the Bible. We go to it searching for simple and clear solutions to our ethical enigmas, but it strikes back exacerbating our perplexity. Who said that the Word of God is supposed to make things easier? But have I not forgotten something? This is an address delivered to bishops, heirs of the Lutheran Reformation. If something distinguishes that tradition, it is its Christological emphasis. *Solus Christus* is one of the main tenets of the Lutheran Reformation. What then about Christ and the stranger?

---

expressed in the stories of Ruth, a "Moabite woman," and the Syro-Phoenician mother who implores Jesus to heal her daughter. Susanna Snyder, *Asylum-Seeking, Migration and Church*, 139–94.

36. Ateek, *Palestinian Christian Cry for Reconciliation*, 132.
37. Trible, *Texts of Terror*.
38. *Welcoming the Stranger*, 85, 98; *Christians at the Border*, 83–84.

Clues to address Jesus' perspective regarding the socially despised other or stranger can be found in his attitude towards the Samaritans and in his dramatic and surprising eschatological parable on genuine discipleship and fidelity (Matthew 25:31–46). Orthodox Jews despised Samaritans as possible sources of contamination and impurity. Yet Jesus did not have any inhibitions in conversing amiably with a Samaritan woman of doubtful reputation, breaking down the exclusion barrier between Judeans and Samaritans (John 4:7–30). Of ten lepers once cleansed by Jesus, only one came to express his gratitude and reverence, and the Gospel narrative emphasizes that "he was a Samaritan" (Luke 17:11–19). Finally, in the famous parable to illustrate the meaning of the command "love your neighbor as yourself" (Luke 10:29–37), Jesus contrasts the righteousness and solidarity of a Samaritan with the neglect and indifference of a priest and a Levite. The action of a traditionally despised Samaritan is thus exalted as a paradigm of love and solidarity to emulate.

The parable of the judgment of the nations, in the Gospel of Matthew (25:31–46), is pure vintage Jesus. It is a text whose connotations I refuse to reduce to a nowadays too common and constraining ecclesiastical confinement. Jesus disrupts, as he loved to do, the familiar criteria of ethical value and religious worthiness by distinguishing between human actions that sacramentally bespeak divine love for the powerless and vulnerable from those that do not. Who are, according to Jesus, to be divinely blessed and inherit God's kingdom? Those who in their actions care for the hungry, thirsty, naked, sick, and incarcerated, in short, for the marginalized and vulnerable human beings. But also those who welcome the strangers, who provide them with hospitality; those who are able to overcome nationalistic exclusions, racism, and xenophobia and are daring enough to welcome and embrace the alien, the people in our midst who happen to be different in skin pigmentation, culture, language, and national origins. They belong to the powerless of the powerless, the poorest of the poor, in Franz Fanon's famous terms, "the wretched of the earth," or, in Jesus's poetic language, "the least of these."[39]

Why? Here comes the shocking statement: because they are, in their powerlessness and vulnerability, the sacramental presence of Christ. "For I was hungry and you gave me food, I was thirsty and you gave me something to drink, I was a stranger [*xénos*] and you welcomed me, I was naked and you gave me clothing, I was sick and you took care of me. . ." (Matthew 25:35). The vulnerable human beings become, in a mysterious way, the

---

39. See Clark Lyda's and Jesse Lyda's moving documentary, *The Least of These* (2009).

sacramental presence of Christ in our midst.⁴⁰ This sacramental presence of Christ becomes, for the first generations of Christian communities, the corner stone of hospitality, *philoxenia*, towards those needy people who do not have a place to rest, a virtue insisted upon by the apostle Paul (Romans 12:13).⁴¹ When, in a powerful and imperial nation, like the United States of America, its citizens welcome and embrace the immigrant, who reside and work with or without some documents required by the powers that be, they are blessed, for they are welcoming and embracing Jesus Christ.⁴²

The discriminatory distinction between citizens and aliens is therefore broken down. The author of the Epistle to the Ephesians is thus able to proclaim to human communities religiously scorned and socially marginalized: "So then you are no longer strangers and aliens, but you are citizens. . ." (Ephesians 2:19). The author of that missive probably had in mind the peculiar vision of post-exilic Israel developed by the prophet Ezekiel. Ezekiel emphasizes two differences between the post-exilic and the old Israel: the eradication of social injustice and oppression ("And my princes shall no longer oppress my people"—Ezekiel 45:8) and the elimination of the legal distinctions between citizens and aliens ("You shall allot it [the land] as an inheritance for yourselves and for the aliens who reside among you and have begotten children among you. They shall be to you as citizens of Israel; with you they shall be allotted an inheritance among the tribes of Israel. In whatever tribe aliens reside, there you shall assign them their inheritance, says the Lord God"—Ezekiel 47:21–23).

AN ECUMENICAL, INTERNATIONAL, AND INTERCULTURAL THEOLOGICAL PERSPECTIVE

We need to countervail the xenophobia that contaminates public discourse in the United States and other Western nations with an embracing,

---

40. Regarding Matthew 25:31–46, I am in accord with those scholars, like Cervantes Gabarrón ("El inmigrante en las tradiciones bíblicas," 273–75) who interpret "the least of these" as referring to the poor, dispossessed, marginalized, and oppressed, and in disagreement with those who limit its denotation to Jesus' disciples, like M. Daniel Carroll R. (*Christians at the Border*, 122–23).

41. Phan, "Migration in the Patristic Age," 35–61.

42. There is an instance in which Jesus seems to exclude or marginalize strangers. When a woman, "Gentile, of Syrophoenician origin," implores from him healing her daughter, Jesus declines. But her obstinate, clever, and hopeful response impresses him and leads him to praise her word of faith (Matthew 15:21–28; Mark 7:24–30).

exclusion-rejecting, perspective of the stranger, the alien, the "other,"[43] one which I have named *xenophilia*, a concept that comprises hospitality, love, and care for the stranger. In times of increasing economic and political globalization, when in a megalopolis like New York, Chicago, London, Madrid, or Paris many different cultures, languages, memories, and legacies converge,[44] *xenophilia* should be our duty and vocation, as a faith affirmation not only of our common humanity, but also of the ethical priority in the eyes of God of those vulnerable beings living in the shadows and margins of our societies.

There is a tendency among many public scholars and leaders to weave a discourse that deals with immigrants mainly or even exclusively as workers, whose labor might contribute or not to the economic welfare of the American citizens. This kind of public discourse tends to objectify and dehumanize the immigrants. Those immigrants are human beings, conceived and designed, according to the Christian tradition, in the image of God. They deserve to be fully recognized as such, both in the letter of the law and in the spirit of social praxis. Whatever the importance of the economical factors for the receiving nation (which usually, as in the case of the United States, happens to be a wealthy country), from an ethical-theological perspective the main concern should be the existential well-being of the "least of these," of the most vulnerable and marginalized members of God's humanity, among them those who sojourn far away from their homeland, constantly scrutinized by the demeaning gaze of many native citizens.

One of the main concerns energizing and spreading the distrust against resident foreigners is fear of their possible consequences on national identity, understood as an already historically fixed essence. We have seen that anxiety in Samuel P. Huntington's assessment of Latin-American immigration as "a major potential threat to the cultural integrity of the United States." It is an apprehension that has spread all over the Western world, disseminating hostile attitudes towards already marginalized and disenfranchised communities of sojourners and strangers. These are perceived as sources of "cultural contamination." What is therein forgotten is, first, that national identities are historical constructs diachronically constituted by exchanges with peoples bearing different cultural heritages and, second, that cultural alterity, the social exchange with the "other," can and should be a source of renewal and enrichment of our own distinct national

---

43. See Volf, *Exclusion and Embrace*.
44. Schweiker, *Theological Ethics and Global Dynamics*.

self-awareness. History has shown the sad consequences of xenophobic ethnocentrism. There have been too intimate links between xenophobia and genocide.[45] As Zygmunt Bauman has so aptly written, "Great crimes often starts from great ideas. . . Among this class of ideas, pride of place belongs to the vision of purity."[46]

The United States has a tendency to play the role of the Lone Ranger. Yet, migration and xenophobia are international problems, affecting most of the world community, and have thus to be understood and faced from a worldwide context. The deportation of Roma people (Gypsies) in France and other European nations is an unfortunate sign of the times. Roma communities are expelled from nations where they are objects of scorn, contempt and fear, to other nations where they have traditionally been mistreated, disdained, and marginalized. They are perennial national scapegoats, whose unfortunate fate has for too long been silenced.[47] It would also do good to compare the American situation with that prevailing in several European nations where in the difficult and sometimes tense coexistence of citizens and immigrants resonate the historically complex conflicts between the Cross and the Crescent, for many of the foreigners happen to be Muslims, venerators of Allah, and thus subject to insidious kinds of xenophobia and discrimination.[48]

Migration is an international problem, a salient dimension of modern globalization.[49] Globalization implies not only the transfer of financial resources, products, and trade, but also the worldwide relocation of peoples, a transnationalization of labor migration, of human beings who take the difficult and frequently painful decision to leave their kin and kith searching for a better future. We are in the midst, according to some scholars, of

---

45. Maalouf, *In the Name of Identity*.

46. Bauman, *Postmodernity and Its Discontents*, 5.

47. See European Commission, "Roma in Europe."

48. Sartori, *Pluralismo, multiculturalismo e estranei*. Sartori perceives Islamist immigration as irreconcilable with, and thus nefarious for, Western democratic pluralism. His thesis is a sophisticated reconfiguration of the multisecular adversary confrontation between Christian/Western (supposedly open, secular, and liberal) and Islamic/Eastern (allegedly closed, dogmatic and authoritarian) cultures, a new reenactment of what Edward Said appropriately named "Orientalism."

49. A task to which not enough attention has been devoted is the advocacy for the signature and ratification by the wealthy and powerful nations of the 1990 "International Convention on the Protection of the Rights of All Migrant Workers and Members of Their Families," which entered into force on July 1, 2003.

an "age of migration."[50] Borders have become bridges, not only barriers. For, as Edward Said has written in the context of another very complex issue, "in time, who cannot suppose that the borders themselves will mean far less than the human contact taking place between people for whom differences animate more exchange rather than more hostility?"[51]

The intensification of global inequalities has made the issue of labor migration a crucial one.[52] It is a situation that requires rigorous analysis from: 1) a worldwide ecumenical horizon; 2) a deep understanding of the tensions and misunderstandings arising from the proximity of peoples with different traditions and cultural memories; 3) an ethical perspective that privileges the plight and afflictions of the most vulnerable, as "submerged and silenced voices of strangers need to be uncovered"[53]; and 4) for the Christian communities and churches, a solid theological matrix ecumenically conceived and designed.

The churches and Christian communities, therefore, need to address this issue from an international ecumenical and intercultural perspective.[54] The main concern is not and should not be exclusively our national society, but the entire fractured global order, for as Soerens and Hwang have neatly written: "Ultimately, the church must be a place of reconciliation in a broken world."[55] In an age where globalization prevails, there are social issues, migration one of them, whose transnational complexities call for an international ecumenical dialogue and debate. As Susanna Snyder has so aptly written, "a transnational issue requires transnational responses and transnational, global networks such as churches could therefore be key international players."[56] One goal of that world-wide discursive process is the

---

50. Castles and Miller, *Age of Migration*.

51. Said, *Question of Palestine*, 176.

52. Some scholars, for example, argue that the North American Free Trade Agreement, which came into force on January 1, 1994, created havoc in several segments of the Mexican economy and deprived of their livelihoods approximately 2.5 million small farmers and other workers dependent on the agricultural sector. The alternative for many of them was the stark choice between the clandestine and dangerous drug trafficking or paying the "coyotes" for the also clandestine and dangerous trek to the North. Ehrenreich, "A Lucrative War," 15–18.

53. Susanna Snyder, *Asylum-Seeking, Migration and Church*, 31.

54. Fornet-Betancourt, *Migration and Interculturality*; Castillo Guerra, "Theology of Migration," 243–70.

55. *Welcoming the Stranger*, 174.

56. *Asylum-Seeking, Migration and Church*, 205.

disruption of the increasing tendency of developed and wealthy countries to emphasize the protection of civil rights, understood exclusively as the rights of *citizens*, vis-à-vis the diminishment of the recognition of the human rights of resident non-citizens.[57]

Pope Benedict XVI rightly reminded the global community, in his 2009 social encyclical *Caritas in veritate*, of the urgent necessity to develop that kind of international and ecumenical perspective of migration:

> [M]igration . . . is a striking phenomenon because of the sheer numbers of people involved, the social, economic, political, cultural and religious problems it raises . . . [We] are facing a social phenomenon of epoch-making proportions that requires bold, forward-looking policies of international cooperation . . . We are all witnesses of the burden of suffering, the dislocation and the aspirations that accompany the flow of migrants . . . [T]hese laborers cannot be considered as a commodity or a mere workforce. They must not, therefore, be treated like any other factor of production. Every migrant is a human person who, as such, possesses fundamental, inalienable rights that must be respected by everyone and in every circumstance.[58]

---

57. Oliván, *El extranjero y su sombra*.
58. *Caritas in veritate*, par. 62.

6

Reading the Hebrew Bible in Solidarity with the Palestinian People[1]

The Bible . . . unlike the books of other ancient peoples, was . . . the literature of a minor, remote people—and not the literature of its rulers, but of its critics. The scribes and the prophets of Jerusalem refused to accept the world as it was. They invented the literature of political dissent and, with it, the literature of hope.

—Amos Elon[2]

UNEARTHING FORGOTTEN MEMORIES

The dreadful plight of the Palestinian nation since the 1948 and 1967 armed victories, military occupation, and territorial expansions of the newly created state of Israel,[3] should be of prime consideration for any theology with

1. Previous versions of this paper were read at the Sixth International Conference "Biblical Texts, Ur-Contexts & Contemporary Realities," organized by the Lutheran International Center, August 8–12, 2011, in Bethlehem, Palestine, and at the International Conference "Violence in the Name of God? Joshua in Changing Contexts," sponsored by the Palestine Israel Ecumenical Forum of the World Council of Churches, February 23–27, 2012, in the Protestant Academy of Hofgeismer, Germany.

2. Elon, *Jerusalem*, 19.

3. Said, *Question of Palestine* and Pappe, *History of Modern Palestine*. For the 1967

emancipatory horizons that truly cares about the sufferings and aspirations of subjugated peoples and victimized communities. As the eminent African-American author Alice Walker has recently noted, after visiting Gaza: "whatever has happened to humanity, whatever is currently happening to humanity, it is happening to all of us. No matter how hidden the cruelty, no matter how far off the screams of pain and terror, we live in one world. We are one people."[4]

The Palestinian situation brings to the fore several crucial theological and hermeneutical issues. The search for justice, liberation and peace is essential to any genuine religious piety. The laureate Jewish-American writer Isaac Bashevis Singer, at the end of his novella *The Penitent*, avers: "There is a great element of protest in all religion. Those who dedicate their lives to serving God have often dared to question His justice, and to rebel against His seeming neutrality in humanity's struggle between good and evil. I feel therefore that there is no basic difference between rebellion and prayer."[5]

My purpose in this essay is to discuss briefly six hermeneutical dilemmas foregrounded by the project of reading the Hebrew sacred scriptures in the context of the actual conflict between Israel and the Palestinian people. They have to do with the following topics: Exodus and conquest; captivity, displacement, and exile; the Promised Land; the chosen people of God; the city of Jerusalem; and, finally, peace and reconciliation.

These conflictual issues are unavoidable if we are to engage in the hermeneutical circle of looking simultaneously and dialectically to both the biblical Hebrew testimonies of faith and the plight of the peoples that presently inhabit Palestine.[6] In the confrontation between Israel and Palestine, this circular and emancipatory hermeneutical perspective is vital due to the frequent reference to the Bible by Israeli intellectuals and political leaders in their quest to devise a transcendentally endowed and legitimized national ethos.[7] According to Anita Shapira, a well-known Israeli scholar, "Zionism ... took the Bible to its heart as the story of the formation of a nation ... The

---

war that forged the military occupation of the Palestinian West Bank, Gaza and East Jerusalem, see Oren, *Six Days of War*.

4. Walker, "Overcoming Speechlessness," 35–36.

5. Singer, *Penitent*, 169. Singer is a magnificent narrator of the Yiddish-speaking communities in Eastern Europe violently wiped out by Nazi anti-Semitism during the Second World War. See his *Collected Stories*.

6. On the concept of hermeneutical circle, see the first chapter of Segundo, *Liberation of Theology*.

7. Masalha, *Bible and Zionism*.

Bible accorded the tender Jewish nationalism the mythic-historical foundation for conceiving the consciousness of the nation's singularity in its bond to the land of the forefathers. In an almost obvious way it [the Bible] served as proof of the 'naturalness' of the Zionist solution for the Jewish problem."[8]

In the interpretative perspective we are adopting, the essential imperative is to remember and radicalize the prophetic words written by the imprisoned Dietrich Bonhöffer, in a note surreptitiously preserved by his friend Eberhard Bethge: "We have for once learnt to see the great events of world history from below, from the perspective of the outcast, the suspects, the maltreated, the powerless, the oppressed, the reviled—in short, from the perspective of those who suffer."[9] This hermeneutical horizon, in constant critical and creative dialogue with contemporary liberation theologies and postcolonial theories,[10] is strikingly analogous to Edward Said's representation of the intellectual as a person who unearths "the memory of forgotten voices . . . of the poor, the disadvantaged, the voiceless, the unrepresented, the powerless."[11] Its original source is an admonition on countless occasions reiterated by the Hebrew Bible, or *Tanakh*, itself:

> Speak out for those who cannot speak,
> for the rights of all the destitute . . .
> defend the rights of the poor and needy.
> (Proverbs 31:8–9)

EXODUS AND CONQUEST

Liberation theologies all over the world have focused on the biblical *Exodus* story as a key emancipatory hermeneutical paradigm.[12] Yet, they have

---

8. Shapira, *Bible and Israeli Identity*, 3, quoted and translated from the Hebrew by Piterberg, *Returns of Zionism,* 195. See also Sand, *Invention of the Jewish People*, 255: "Jewish nationalism had undertaken an almost impossible mission—to forge a single *ethnos* from a great variety of cultural-linguistic groups, each with a distinctive origin. This accounts for the adoption of the Old Testament as the storehouse of national memory."

9. Bonhöffer, *Letters and Papers from Prison*, 16.

10. Relevant in this context is Fernando Segovia's sharp and critical exposition of the theoretical convergences between postcolonial studies and anti-imperial biblical hermeneutics: "Mapping the Postcolonial Optic in Biblical Criticism," in Moore and Segovia, *Postcolonial Biblical Criticism*, 23–78. Regarding Palestinian biblical hermeneutics, see Segovia's extended essay, "Engaging the Palestinian Theological-Critical Project of Liberation," in *Biblical Text in the Context of Occupation*, edited by Raheb, 29–80, 395–399.

11. Said, *Representations of the Intellectuals*, 35, 113.

12. Croatto, *Exodus, a Hermeneutics of Freedom* and Pixley, *On Exodus*.

Reading the Hebrew Bible in Solidarity with the Palestinian People

usually evaded the sinister dimensions of its accompanying story: the conquest of Canaan and its concomitant destruction of the Canaanite communities.[13] Edward Said noticed this omission ("the injunction laid on the Jews by God to exterminate their opponents") in a critical review of Michael Walzer's much-read book *Exodus and Revolution*,[14] which he indicts as "so undialectical, so simplifying, so ahistorical and reductive."[15] The exalting view of the biblical Exodus as a process of redemption of the Hebrew slaves oftentimes eludes the ethnic cleansing and massacre of the indigenous Canaanites, as narrated in the biblical book of *Joshua*, and "minimizes, if it does not completely obliterate, a sense of responsibility for what a people undergoing Redemption does to other less fortunate people, unredeemed, strange, displaced and outside moral concern."[16] This critical perspective might lead to read the Exodus/conquest biblical narratives "with the eyes of the Canaanites."[17]

Palestinian theological hermeneutics is able to foreground this usually silenced, ominous dimension of the Exodus story, both in its biblical context—the atrocious rules of warfare that prescribed forced servitude or annihilation for the population encountered in Israel's route to the "promised land" (Deuteronomy 20:10-17)—and in the present historical circumstances wherein the Palestinian communities are harshly mistreated by the state of Israel. From a Palestinian perspective, the Exodus story can be read contrapuntally, the way that Edward Said, for example, analyses Albert Camus's occlusion of Algeria and the Algerians in several of his most important literary texts (*La Peste*, *L'Étranger*), though they take place in that specific Maghreb nation.[18]

In the biblical narrative of the Israelite invasion and conquest of Canaan, the indigenous communities were perceived as potential sources of

13. One notable exception was the late Irish priest and theologian Prior. See his essay "Confronting the Bible's Ethnic Cleansing In Palestine," 1–12.

14. Walzer, *Exodus and Revolution*.

15. Said, "Michael Walzer's 'Exodus and Revolution,'" 91, 96.

16. Ibid., 104–5. Said's review led to a bitter and acrimonious exchange between both eminent intellectuals [Walzer and Said, "An Exchange: 'Exodus and Revolution,'" 246–259] which ends with the following denigrating comments by Said: "Walzer's extraordinarily myopic and ungenerous *envoi* . . . is little more than a catalogue of his qualifications for prolonged servility to a strong Israel. A courtier, an amateur mythographer, a champion of the strong. A small frightened man who is completely unequal to the question of Canaan-Palestine, and barely adequate for the easier bits of Exodus."

17. Prior, "Reading the Bible with the Eyes of the Canaanites," 273–296.

18. Said, *Culture and Imperialism*, 66–67, 169–85.

ethnic, religious, and ethical contamination. The Hebrew tribes claimed divine right to displace, expel, and exterminate them: "As for the towns of these peoples that the Lord your God is giving you as an inheritance, you must not let anything that breathes remain alive. You shall annihilate them . . . just as the Lord your God has commanded" (Deuteronomy 20:16f).[19] A similar commandment is given to King Saul regarding the complete extermination of Amalek: "Now go and attack Amalek, and utterly destroy all that they have; do not spare them, but kill both man and woman, child and infant, ox and sheep, camel and donkey" (1 Samuel 15:3). The divine mandate is to destroy even the historical remembrance of its existence: "You must blot out the memory of Amalek under heaven. Do not forget" (Deuteronomy 25:19). Saul provokes God's wrath by not fulfilling completely this genocidal decree. Regarding the Midian kingdom, the divine order is to kill all its male inhabitants, including "the little ones," and all the women who have "known a man by sleeping with him" (Numbers 31:17). Only the "young girls who have not known a man by sleeping with him" are to be spared. The narration of the massacre of the inhabitants of Jericho is chilling and dreadful: "Then they devoted to destruction by the edge of the sword all in the city, both men and women, young and old. . ." (Joshua 6:21).[20] The God of grace, blessing, and redemption mutates into the God of wrath, curse, and devastation.[21]

Later biblical texts will attempt to explain and justify the annihilation of those peoples adducing their intertwined vices of idolatry and moral aberration. "For the idea of making idols was the beginning of fornication, and the invention of them was the corruption of life" (Wisdom of Solomon 14:12; see also 12:3–7 and 14:27). The purpose of these vindictive texts and genocidal commandments is to protect Israel from possible contamination

---

19. Due to constrains of space, I am sidelining an important issue: recent archaeological studies have undermined the historicity of the Exodus/Conquest biblical narrative. See Finkelstein and Silberman, *The Bible Unearthed*. Their general conclusion is that the new archeological discoveries "have cast serious doubts on the historical basis for such famous biblical stories as the wanderings of the patriarchs, the Exodus from Egypt and conquest of Canaan, and the glorious empire of David and Solomon" (3).

20. The biblical narrative destruction of Jericho ends with a solemn curse against whoever might attempt to rebuild the city (Joshua 6:26). Jericho, however, has been able to survive its too many catastrophes and curses, as anybody who has visited it can verify.

21. I am well aware that these genocidal commandments are theological and literary constructions and that such heinous acts of genocide did not take place as narrated. But the fact that they were inscribed in the Bible gave them a sacred authoritative status to be misemployed in posterior conflicts between "believers" and "infidels."

by the collusion of religious impurity and moral perversion prevailing in the Canaanite nations. It constitutes a divine declaration of anathema (*herem*) against peoples whose impurity might pollute God's elected nation. An analogous attitude can be found in the process of reconstructing Jerusalem and the temple, as narrated by Ezra 9–10 and Nehemiah 13:23–30, resulting in the merciless expulsion of the foreign wives and their children in service of the xenophobic principle of ethnic purity as an absolute prerequisite for moral integrity and religious fidelity.[22] These are truly, in Phyllis Trible's apt phrase, texts of terror.[23]

Dreadful resonances of this lethal and discriminatory outlook are found in the writings of some Spanish theologians and jurists during the sixteenth-century Iberian conquest of the Americas,[24] in several admonitions of British theologians regarding the Native Americans of North America,[25] in the way certain South African Boer preachers looked at Black Africans, as well as in the proclamations of many contemporary Zionists who quote those biblical texts to legitimate their aspiration for a Greater Israel (Eretz Israel) sanitized from any possible "contamination" by Palestinians.[26]

The Hebrew Bible is thus transformed into a sacred vindicating source for the aspiration of Eretz Israel, as a divinely awarded patrimony exclusively for the Jewish people, which also legitimates the dispossession of the new Canaanites, the Palestinians. The *Tanakh*, in this interpretative scheme, plays a twin role: it serves to construe the unity of the nation of Israel across millennia, from Abraham to David Ben-Gurion, and it gives to that national community exclusive proprietary rights over the land of Canaan/Palestine. The ultimate goal of this specific hermeneutics might just be to masquerade ethnic cleansing and displacement with a prestigious Biblical justification. As Nur Masalha, a distinguished Palestinian scholar and writer, has affirmed: "Inspired by a fundamentalist interpretation of the Old Testament, especially the books of Exodus, Deuteronomy and Joshua,

---

22. A recent first-rate study of these texts of Ezra and Nehemiah on the expulsion of the foreign wives has been written by Cook Steicke, *La mujer como extranjera en Israel*.

23. Trible, *Texts of Terror*.

24. Rivera-Pagán, *Violent Evangelism*.

25. Bosch, *Transforming Mission*, 275: "To subdue them [the original inhabitants of North America] and take their land was regarded as a divine duty similar to the Israelites' conquest of Canaan; on occasion I Samuel 15:3 could be applied directly to the colonists' conflict with the Indians—'Now go and smite Amalek, and utterly destroy all that they have...'"

26. See Akenson, *God's Peoples* and Prior, *Bible and Colonialism*.

their discourse [the Zionists'] presents ethnic cleansing as not only legitimate, but as required by the divinity."[27] The Bible trumps, in this perspective, the second part of the 1917 Balfour Declaration that committed the British government to "the establishment in Palestine of a national home for the Jewish people . . . it being clearly understood that nothing shall be done which may prejudice the civil and religious rights of existing non-Jewish communities . . ."[28]

We are, thus, obliged to consider carefully and critically the ominous dimensions of the Exodus biblical narratives if we are to be faithful to the divine covenant of doing righteousness and pursuing justice. Otherwise, one might be complicit in evading the nefarious narrative proximity of the Exodus story to the tragic fate of the indigenous population inhabiting "the promised land that flows with milk and honey."

CAPTIVITY, DISPLACEMENT, AND EXILE

From the painful memory of the *al-nakba* (the "great catastrophe"), Palestinian theology is able to highlight the biblical topoi of exile, displacement, dispersion, and captivity, the crucial historical matrices of the biblical scriptures, as meaningful loci of theological enunciation and reflection. The heart-breaking experience of devastation, dispersion, and dislocation are at the core of the Hebrew sacred scriptures.

> How lonely sits the city
> that once was full of people!
> How like a widow she has become,
> she that was great among the nations!
> . . .
> Judah has gone into exile with suffering
> And hard servitude;
> She lives now among the nations,
> And finds no resting place.
>
> (Lamentations 1:1, 3)

Many texts of the Hebrew Bible apparently were composed, edited and reconfigured after the traumatic experience of the Babylonian exile. It is from the sufferings entailed by national defeat, devastation, the

27. Masalha, *Bible and Zionism*, 157.
28. I am quoting the Balfour Declaration from Prior, *Zionism and the State of Israel*, 13.

destruction of the holy places, and exile (*galut*)[29] that the biblical sacred scriptures emerge, fueled by the need and desire to remember, to preserve the memory of God as the ultimate source of liberation and of the desperate but obstinate hope for a peaceful return to the lost homeland.[30] Contrary to other ancient Middle East sacred scriptures, written by courtly scribes and characterized by their laudatory paeans to the national authorities, the Bible arises from the tragic experience of exile and captivity and evokes the flaws and misdeeds of the Israelite and Judean monarchs. They are sacred scriptures precisely because they surge and arise from a displaced people, who recall with profound sadness the devastation of their homes and places of worship and their forceful uprooting, but that do not abdicate their divinely inspired hopes for restitution. Exile, deportation, and captivity become the subterranean sources of liberative theological meditation and creativity of the remembrance of God as the Liberator.[31]

In the Gospel According to Luke, Jesus's vision of the coming destruction of Jerusalem and the painful displacement and dispossession of its inhabitants, after the defeat of the Jewish rebellion against the Romans (66—70 CE), is constantly alluded to as a reason for his profound sadness, who mourns with heart-breaking lamentations the tragic fate of the people: "As he [Jesus] came near and saw the city [Jerusalem], he wept over it . . . the days will come upon you, when your enemies will set up ramparts around you and surround you, and hem you on every side. They will crush you to the ground, you and your children within you, and they will not leave within you one stone upon another . . ." (Luke 19:41–44). Defeat, exile, and dispersion constitute, therefore, the historical matrices also for the New Testament, the Christian sacred scriptures.[32]

---

29. The Hebrew word *galut* expresses the condition and feelings of the Jewish people uprooted from their homeland and subject to alien rule. The term is essentially applied to the history and the historical consciousness of the Jewish people from the destruction of the Temple to the creation of the State of Israel. According to Zionist orthodoxy, the loss of a political-ethnic center and the feeling of uprootedness turn Diaspora (*Golah*) into Exile (*galut*).

30. Smith-Christopher, *Biblical Theology of Exile*.

31. See Steiner, "Our Homeland, the Text," 304–27; Wit, *En la dispersión el texto es patria*; and Boff, *Teología desde el cautiverio*.

32. One must be aware, however, that Luke's interpretation of the destruction of Jerusalem and the defeat of the Jewish revolt against the Roman Empire, as divine punishment for the rejection of Jesus by the Jews and his crucifixion (Luke 19:44; 21:20–23), would become an important leitmotif for Christian anti-Judaism. Eusebius of Caesarea, for example, wrote, regarding the devastation of Jerusalem and the Temple in 70 CE:

Essays from the Margins

It has been an expatriate Palestinian, Edward Said, who with his typical literary eloquence, has described, like perhaps nobody else since the biblical psalmist, the plight and grief of exile, the painful dilemma of displacement: "Exile is strangely compelling to think about but terrible to experience. It is the unhealable rift forced between a human being and a native place, between the self and its true home: its essential sadness can never be surmounted."[33] It situates the exiled person in a strange situation of being perennially "out of place," to refer to the title of Said's personal memoir.[34]

Israeli policy on Palestine has been neatly encapsulated in the formula "maximum land and minimum Arabs." The deportation and removal of the Palestinians has been a tragic but almost historically unavoidable consequence of the ideological structure of Jewish Zionism as a theological colonial nationalism. Those who for almost two millennia suffered the plight of exclusion and disdain, in their national resurgence and quest for a homeland have become, paradoxically and ironically, the perpetrators of new acts of dispersion and exile. And they do it in the name of their sacred traditions and their heritage of perseverance in the difficult predicament of diasporic displacement.

The Zionists' various strategies of dispossession and expulsion (usually sweet-termed as "transfer") have been radical: their goal has been not only to reclaim what they consider Israel's ancestral homeland, not only to dislodge the Arab indigenes, but something deeper: to erase the memory of the former presence of the ousted communities, to eliminate all the vestiges of a non-Israeli Palestine. The Palestinian indigenous inhabitants were expelled, their houses looted, destroyed or appropriated, their agricultural fields confiscated, their holy places desecrated. A cartographic discourse of Hebraization and Judaization was systematically put into place to obliterate traces and remnants from the Palestinian birthplace and to establish a new hegemonic experience of the land, intimately associated with Hebrew biblical resonances.[35] Its intended objective was to eradicate the Palestinian people's historical ties with its homeland, truly an ideologically motivated

---

"Thus the penalty of God pursued the Jews for their crimes against Christ." *Ecclesiastical History*, Vol. I, Book II, chapter 6, 125. Such a Judeophobic theology of divine vengeance would reap horrendous consequences in the twentieth century.

33. Said, *Reflections on Exile*, 173.

34. Said, *Out of Place*.

35. See the study of such a process by the Israeli scholar and politician (he was deputy mayor of Jerusalem in the seventies) Benenisti, *Sacred Landscape*.

Reading the Hebrew Bible in Solidarity with the Palestinian People

memoricide. As Ilan Pappe, the dissident Israeli historian, has asserted: "The human geography of Palestine as a whole was forceably transformed ... This transformation was driven by the desire to wipe out one nation's history and culture."[36] Palestine is a palimpsest of memories wherein Israeli leaders pretend to inscribe an exclusive Jewish narrative, wistfully reconnected to the biblical geography and history, while simultaneously trying to occlude all the remnants and vestiges of the centuries-old former Arab communities. That project of erasure, however, is not always totally successful, as Hanna Musleh's fine documentary film *Memory of the Cactus—A Story of Three Palestinian Villages* (2008) so graphically demonstrates.

Exile, an important feature of human historical experience and a vital source of the biblical sacred scriptures, becomes in Palestine a crucial philosophical and theological concern. Exile is, in the poetic words of Mahmoud Darwish, a "journal of an ordinary grief."[37] In many Palestinian hearts and souls the nostalgic sadness inscribed in Darwish's verses resonates with uncanny familiarity:

> There is no place on earth where we haven't pitched our tent of exile ...
> Longing is the place of exile. Our love is a place of exile.
> Our wine is a place of exile
> and a place of exile is the history of this heart.
> How many times have we told the trees
> of the place to wipe off the invader's mask
> so we might find a place? ...
> Poetry is a place of exile.
> (I See What I Want to See).[38]

THE PROMISED LAND

The geographical territory that Christians traditionally call Holy Land,[39] Muslims name Palestine, and Jews designate as Israel, has been during

---

36. Pappe, *Ethnic Cleansing of Palestine*, 216. I am borrowing the term "memoricide" from Pappe, ibid., 225–34.

37. Darwish, *Journal of an Ordinary Grief*.

38. Darwish, *Unfortunately, It Was Paradise*, 42–43.

39. Only in Zechariah 2:12 is the expression "holy land" found in the Hebrew Bible. "The Lord will inherit Judah as his portion in the holy land..." (NRSV) In Roman Catholic versions this verse is usually located in Zechariah 2:16: "Yahweh will take possession of Judah, his portion in the Holy Land..." (NJB)

many centuries a source of passionate and violent conflicts, truly a land of blood and tears.[40] In the name of Yahweh, Allah, or Christ, ferocious warriors have bitterly clashed and fought for its possession and dominion.

God's promise of the land of Canaan to Abraham, according to the Hebrew sacred scriptures, is a basic tenet of the Zionist claim that the entire land of Palestine belongs by divine right to the Jewish people, more precisely to Israel as the Jewish state.[41] Genesis 12:1–7 ("To your offspring I will give this land"), 15:18–21 ("To your descendants I give this land"), and 17:1–8 ("I will give to you, and to your offspring, the land where your are now an alien, all the land of Canaan, for a perpetual holding...") reproduce several versions of God's promise to Abraham that Canaan will be the everlasting possession of his progeny. This is the biblical mythical/historical basis for Israel's claim of proprietary rights over the land of Palestine.[42] As Hanan Porat, one of the founders of the Gush Emunim ("Bloc of the Faithful") movement and a conservative Israeli politician, once asserted: "For us the Land of Israel is a Land of destiny, a chosen Land . . . It is the Land from which the voice of God has called to us ever since that first call to the first Hebrew: 'Come and go forth from your Land where you were born and from your father's house to the Land that I will show you.'"[43]

There is, however, an inner paradoxical tension in this biblical divine promise. Supposedly, in its fulfillment "all the families of the earth shall be blessed" (Genesis 12:3); yet many communities and nations already inhabit the land where Abraham is "now an alien." What, then, might be the fate of the peoples and nations that are supposed to be blessed by the conquest and perpetual occupation of their land by Abraham's descendants?

---

40. See Brueggemann, *Land*, and more recently, from Jerusalem itself, Marchadour and Neuhaus, *Land, the Bible, and History*.

41. I have in mind the Jewish political Zionism as well as the fundamentalist and apocalyptic Christian Zionism, so widespread in Anglo-Saxon Evangelical circles. On the first, with its sometimes convergent, sometimes divergent inner trends, see Piterberg, *Returns of Zionism*. On the second, Sizer, *Christian Zionism* and Smith, *More Desired than Our Owne Salvation*. A brief but very precise and enlightening summary of the different kinds of Jewish Zionism is provided by Ruether and Ruether, *Wrath of Jonah*, 39–67.

42. The definition of the exact boundaries of the allegedly divinely "promised land" constitutes a tortuous exegetical debate among different Zionist factions. The most extremist position, on the basis of Genesis 15:18 ("from the river of Egypt [the Nile] to the great river, the river of Euphrates"), claims, as belonging to Eretz Israel, extensive territories belonging today to several neighboring Arab nations.

43. Quoted by Nur Masalha, *Bible & Zionism*, 138.

Reading the Hebrew Bible in Solidarity with the Palestinian People

The dispossession of the Palestinians has been defended by attributing to them the alleged decadence and defilement of the land before its redeeming Jewish colonization. The Promised Land has been transmogrified, according to this argument, into a Wasted Land. Mark Twain's pejorative description of Palestine, included in his book *The Innocents Abroad* (1869), has been quoted by several Israeli leaders to justify the displacement of the indigenous population.

> Palestine sits in sackcloth and ashes. Over it broods the spell of a curse that has withered its fields and fettered its energies . . . Bethlehem and Bethany, in their poverty and their humiliation, have nothing about them now to remind one that they once knew the high honor of the Savior's presence . . . Renowned Jerusalem itself, the stateliest name in history, has lost all its ancient grandeur, and is become a pauper village; the riches of Solomon are no longer there to compel the admiration of visiting Oriental queens; the wonderful temple which was the pride and the glory of Israel, is gone . . . Palestine is desolate and unlovely. And why should it be otherwise? Can the curse of the Deity beautify a land?[44]

When Theodor Herzl, one of the main founders of political Zionism, wrote, in *The Jewish State*, "Palestine is our unforgettable historic homeland,"[45] two conflicting perspectives were brought to a horizon of violent confrontation. On one side, the Jewish people, scattered, ghettoed, and disdained in the melancholy of exile, forever preserving in their Diaspora (*Golah*) the memory of Zion as its birthright homeland by divine concession and liturgically proclaiming annually that they will gather again "next year in Jerusalem."[46] On the other, the indigenous Arab inhabitants of Palestine, perpetual victims of successive foreign empires, upholding their

---

44. Accessed in http://classiclit.about.com/library/bl-etexts/mtwain/bl-mtwain-innocents-56.htm. Twain visited Palestine in 1867 and his travel book *The Innocents Abroad*, published in 1869, was one of his most widely read writings.

45. Quoted by Marchadour and Neuhaus, *Land, the Bible, and History*, 127.

46. The Declaration of the Establishment of the State of Israel (May 14, 1948) begins thus: "ERETZ-ISRAEL [the Land of Israel, Palestine] was the birthplace of the Jewish people. Here their spiritual, religious and political identity was shaped. Here they first attained to statehood, created cultural values of national and universal significance and gave to the world the eternal Book of Books. After being forcibly exiled from their land, the people kept faith with it throughout their Dispersion and never ceased to pray and hope for their return to it and for the restoration in it of their political freedom." See the entire Declaration in http://www.mfa.gov.il/MFA/Peace+Process/Guide+to+the+Peace+Process/Declaration+of+Establishment+of+State+of+Israel.htm.

profound sense of ancestral belonging and who could also claim, "Palestine is our unforgettable historic homeland." Whose, then, is the Promised Land? As it happens so many times in human history, that question has received contradictory answers, supported simultaneously by deeply rooted religious convictions and aggressive military strategies.

Palestinian theologians have been able to respond critically to the employment of the Hebrew Bible to justify Israel's policies of appropriation and exclusion, under the theological pretext that Palestine is supposedly the land promised by God to its biblical ancestors. After all, it is impossible to evade or sideline the prophetic core of the Hebrew sacred scriptures, with their indissoluble linkage of the knowledge of God and the deeds of justice (Jeremiah 22:16) and its emphasis on solidarity and compassion with the most vulnerable sectors of society—the poor, the widows, the orphans, the strangers (Jeremiah 7:4–7)—as the main expression of faithful obedience to God's will.

According to the Hebrew Torah and prophets, the possession of the land is indissolubly connected with a covenant between its inhabitants and God: a pact of justice, mercifulness and solidarity. The violation of that covenant forfeits the right to posses the land. All the biblical narratives, be they juridical, historical, or prophetic, strongly express God's disavowal of Israel's endemic structures of social injustice and, therefore, call their hearers/readers to engage in resistance against them.

How can the *Tanakh* be quoted to justify the aggressive military actions of the actual state of Israel when those same sacred scriptures constantly rebuke and condemn the authorities of biblical Israel due to its unjust policies and oppressive actions? Compare the condemnation of king Jehoiakim in 2 Chronicles 36:5 ("He did what was evil in the sight of the LORD his God") with Jeremiah's invective against the same monarch's social policies: "your eyes and heart are only . . . for practicing oppression and violence" (Jeremiah 22:17). Both critical assessments take place under the shadow of the ominous Chaldean threat, perceived by the scribes in charge of narrating the history of Israel as a divine punishment against that nation's oppressive social structures (2 Chronicles 36:14–17). As Walter J. Houston has noted, "This is the point on which the logic of the prophetic rhetoric pivots. YHWH destroys oppressors; the oppressors denounced in the oracles of judgment were representative of the Israelite kingdoms; this accounts, in the structure of the prophetic books as wholes, for the downfall of those kingdoms."[47] According to the Old Testament scholar Jorge Pixley, of the thirty-nine kings of Israel and Judah mentioned in the biblical chronicles of the two separated kingdoms, only one, Josiah, is considered to do "what is right in the sight of the LORD" (2 Kings 22:2).[48]

There is a dialectical relationship between the biblical promise of land and the communal commitment to justice. As Alain Marchadour and David Neuhaus have appropriately written: "*mishpat* [justice] and *tsedaka* [doing righteousness] . . . summarize the requirements for living out God's will on the Land and they bear witness against and denounce the violations that are too often committed by Israel."[49] They are probably right when they emphasize that the issues at stake in the prophetic denunciations of Israel's conduct "have less to do with offenses committed against God . . . than with injustices inflicted on the poor . . ."[50]

THE CHOSEN PEOPLE OF GOD

The self-designation of Israel as God's chosen people, with exclusive propietary rights over the "promised land," claims biblical foundations. "The Lord said to Abram: 'Go from your country and your father's house to the land that I will show you. I will make of you a great nation . . .' So Abram went [to Canaan], as the Lord had told him . . . Then the Lod appeared to Abram, and said, 'To your offsprings I will give this land'" (Genesis 12:1–2, 4, 7). This is evidently an etiological narrative; it is an account of the origin of a special people, the people of God. But the question arises: Who are the authentic descendants of that wandering Aramean, ancestor of a divinely "chosen people"?

In Palestine, two conflicting views regarding this matter clash. Many Zionists allege that the Jews, wherever they are, and whatever their ethnic, cultural, or linguistic heritage (Ashkenazi or Sephardic; Yiddish, Russian, or Arabic speakers), constitute the elected nation endowed with the divinely decreed legal obligations (the *Halakhah*) and privileges (mainly the possession of Palestine, as Eretz Israel). They comprise a privileged genealogy of the biblical patriarchs. Israel's laws of return and nationality are based upon

---

47. Houston, *Contending for Justice*, 94.
48. Pixley, *Biblia, teología de la liberación y filosofía procesual*, 24.
49. Marchadour and Neuhaus, *Land, the Bible, and History*, 19.
50. Ibid., 76.

this premise of an ethnological distinction.[51] The term ethnocracy has been coined to describe this perspective.[52] This is, in the words of Shlomo Sand, "the active myth of an eternal nation [Israel] that must ultimately forgather in its ancestral land."[53] God's promises to Abraham, Isaac and Jacob are perceived as a divine legitimizing source for Israel's charter of exclusive national privilege for the Jewish people, but also as the transcendental justification for the displacement and opprobrium suffered by the Palestinians.

The history of Israel, from this perspective, is transfigured in a series of constructed narratives devoid of the disturbing presence of the Palestinian indigenous communities. The Palestinian indigenes are occluded, for they do not to belong to God's elected nation. They are not only displaced from their homeland; they are dislodged also from true history, or at least from the historical drama that occurs between God, the divinely chosen people, and the Promised Land, as construed by so many Israeli scholars and politicians.

A new people of God, the *Sabras*, the New Jews, are conceived as the only genuine historical agents in the "redeemed" land of Ancient Israel. The history of the "Others," of the Palestinian communities is marginalized, silenced.[54] Not only is their land confiscated, their bodies expelled, and their civic rights curtailed; their historical memory is also expunged, excised.

51. Israel's 1950 Law of Return and its posterior amendments can be accessed and read in http://www.mfa.gov.il/MFA/MFAArchive/1950_1959/Law+of+Return+5710-1950.htm and the 1952 Nationality Law in http://www.israellawresourcecenter.org/israellaws/fulltext/nationalitylaw.htm. See Edward Said's critical appraisal: "Whereas any Jew anywhere is entitled to Israel citizenship under the Law of Return, no Palestinian anywhere, whether born in Palestine before 1948 or not, has any such right. I refer here to over two million Palestinian refugees, those people (with their recent descendants) who like the Canaanites were originally driven out of their native land by Israel on the premise that they were 'explicitly excluded from the world of moral concern.'" Said, "Michael Walzer's 'Exodus and Revolution': A Canaanite Reading," 103.

52. See Yiftachel, *Ethnocracy: Land and Identity in Israel/Palestine*.

53. *Invention of the Jewish People*, 22.

54. On the diverse ways in which the history of a colonized people is marginalized and silenced, see Trouillot, *Silencing the Past*. Regarding Palestine, see the significant critical study by Whitelam, *Invention of Ancient Israel: The Silencing of Palestinian History*. Whitelam indicts Western biblical scholarship of complicity in the academic silencing of non-Israelite Palestinian history. "[It] has been silenced and excluded by the dominant discourse in biblical studies . . . Biblical studies is, thereby, implicated in an act of dispossession which has its modern political counterpart in the Zionist possession of the land and dispossession of its inhabitants. As a people without history—or deprived of that history by the discourse of biblical studies—they become unimportant, irrelevant, and finally, non-existent" (3, 46).

The dominant collective narrator tries to impede or expunge other alternate and subaltern narratives.[55] Or, at least, that seems to be the prevailing project of identity politics in mainstream Israel, especially after the decline of the old socialist and leftist ideological dimensions of Zionism.

There is, however, a second and different perspective. The biblical references to God's liberation of the Israelites, after hearing their lamentations and woes as an oppressed people in Egypt ["When the Egyptians treated us harshly and afflicted us, by imposing hard labor on us, we cried to the . . . God of our ancestors; the Lord heard our voice and saw our affliction . . . and our oppression" Deuteronomy 26:6], do not necessarily emphasize an alleged biological ancestry. Its crucial point is that there was an enslaved, subjugated, and exploited people and that God, after paying compassionate attention to their sorrowful cries, liberates that people. The concept of "chosen people of God," therefore, does not allude to an absurd DNA genetic analysis, or ethno-racial lineage.[56] It rather evokes a hermeneutic of oppression and liberation. The people of God are those who oppressed, in a seemingly hopeless situation, pray, hope, and struggle for liberation and redemption.[57] What happens in Palestine is a reenactment of the traditional confrontation between two different perspectives: the consciousness of the victors and the consciousness of the victims. In a complex historical irony, "the classic victims of years of anti-Semitic persecution and the Holocaust have in their new nation become the victimizers of another people, who have become, therefore, the victims of the victims."[58] But the Bible, let us not forget, tells the story of a God who stands with the victims against their victimizers.

Shlomo Sand, the Israeli dissident scholar, has asked a pertinent question: "To what extent is Jewish Israeli society willing to discard the deeply embedded image of the 'chosen people' and to cease . . . excluding the 'other' from its midst?"[59] This change might be required not only to strengthen the democratic character of Israeli society, which is Sand's objective, but

---

55. "The power to narrate, or to block other narratives from forming and emerging is very important. . ." Said, *Culture and Imperialism*, xiii.

56. See Shlomo Sand's trenchant critique of the "Jewish genetics" claiming scientific credentials in several Israeli universities. *Invention of the Jewish People*, 256–80.

57. See Ellis, *Toward a Jewish Theology of Liberation*; Ateek, *Justice and Only Justice*; Dabashi, *Islamic Liberation Theology*; Prior, *Jesus the Liberator: Nazareth Liberation Theology*.

58. Said, *Question of Palestine*, xxi.

59. *Invention of the Jewish People*, 312f.

also and mainly to deepen its ethical texture. Reinhold Niebuhr contrasted, in a North American theological classic text, "moral man" with "immoral society,"[60] but God's Torah, according to the Hebrew prophets, requires a social life according to the strict norms of *mishpat* and *tsedaka*, justice and righteousness.[61] It prescribes a "moral society," a society where solidarity and compassion constitute the main rules for judging the conduct of the authority and power. Belonging to God's "chosen people," therefore, is not a privilege or a badge of honor, but rather a difficult to satisfy and formidable challenge, as the prophet Amos hinted when he told Israel:

> You only I have known
> of all the families of the earth;
> therefore I will punish you
> for all your iniquities.
>
> (Amos 3:2)

The sacred scriptures have always proved to be a perilous minefield for all those who attempt to use it to legitimize or justify acts of conquest, domination, or exploitation.[62] As the Israeli writer Amos Elon has eloquently emphasized: "The Bible . . . unlike the books of other ancient peoples, was . . . the literature of a minor, remote people—and not the literature of its rulers, but of its critics. The scribes and the prophets of Jerusalem refused to accept the world as it was. They invented the literature of political dissent and, with it, the literature of hope."[63]

Decades ago, the German Marxist philosopher Ernst Bloch asserted provocatively that reading the Bible should be an imperative for every one whose life is devoted to the quest of liberty and justice for the oppressed.[64] To the astonishment of many Marxists, he insisted upon the basic prophetic and subversive character of the Bible. Bloch's heterodox assessment of the revolutionary potentialities of the Bible was written before the books usually considered as originators of liberation theology, authored by James Cone, Gustavo Gutiérrez, or Hugo Assmann, were published. This is the hermeneutical key to recognize the authentic people of God. For, as

---

60. Niebuhr, *Moral Man and Immoral Society*.

61. "The terms *mishpat* (justice) and *tsedaka* (righteousness) appear together about thirty times in the Bible." Marchadour and Neuhaus, *Land, the Bible, and History*, 49.

62. Horsley, *In the Shadow of Empire*; Gottwald, *Bible and Liberation*.

63. Elon, *Jerusalem*, 19.

64. Bloch, *Atheismus im Christentum*.

Gutiérrez has affirmed: "The entire Bible, beginning with the story of Cain and Abel, mirrors God's predilection for the weak and abused of human history."[65] God's truly chosen people, therefore, is defined not by genetic inheritance, but by obedience of the divine command:

> Give justice to the weak and the orphan;
> maintain the right of the lowly and the destitute.
> Rescue the weak and the needy;
> deliver them from the hand of the wicked.
>
> (Psalm 82:3–4)

Israel's Zionists reiterate emphatically the restorative promise of Amos 9:14f:

> I will restore the fortunes of my people Israel,
> and they shall rebuild the ruined cities and inhabit them;
> they shall plant vineyards and drink their wine,
> and they shall make gardens and eat their fruit.
> I will plant them upon their land,
> and they shall never again be plucked up
> out of their land that I have given them,
> says the Lord your God.

But they tend to silence and occlude the severe critiques that same prophet Amos utters against Israel for her deeds of wickedness and injustice, actions that nullify its self-designation as "God's chosen people."

JERUSALEM, SACRED AND SANGUINARY

As Naim Ateek has underscored, "the history of Jerusalem has been written with blood."[66] In its long and tempestuous history, Jerusalem has been both blessed and cursed due to its recognition as sacred by the three Abrahamic monotheistic religions (Judaism, Islam and Christianity). For centuries they have considered it a "holy city," sanctified by the divine presence. Medieval cosmography and cartography situated Jerusalem as both the geographical and spiritual center of the world. It was perceived as the navel (*omphalos*) of the world, the *axis mundi*.[67] This tradition arose from a literal reading

---

65. Gutiérrez, *Theology of Liberation*, xxvii.

66. Ateek, *Palestinian Christian Cry for Reconciliation*, 140.

67. The 1581 Heinrich Bunting's cloverleaf map still depicts Jerusalem as the *axis mundi* unifying Europe, Asia, and Africa, when traditional medieval cartographic was already outdated by the new discoveries.

of Ezekiel 5:5—"Thus says the Lord God: This is Jerusalem; I have set her in the center of the nations, with countries all around her." The following verse, however, indicates the conflictive character of the history of this most holy city: "But she has rebelled against my ordinances and my statutes, becoming more wicked than the nations and the countries all around her, rejecting my ordinances and not following my statutes" (Ezekiel 5:6). The blessed sacred city of God has become, so is the prophetic judgment, a cursed city of sin, where corruption and injustice prevails,

> How the faithful city
> has become a whore! . . .
> Your princes are rebels
> and companions of thieves.
> Everyone loves a bribe
> and runs after gifts.
> They do not defend the orphan,
> and the widow's cause does not come before them.
>
> (Isaiah 1:21, 23)

Jeremiah's admonitory words regarding the mystification of the Temple are, in this context, unforgettable: "Hear the word of the Lord, all you people of Judah, you that enter these gates to worship the Lord. Thus says the Lord of hosts, the God of Israel: Amend your ways and your doings, and let me dwell with you in this place. Do not trust in these deceptive words: 'This is the temple of the Lord, the temple of the Lord, the temple of the Lord'" (Jeremiah 7:2-4). If the religious rituals and liturgical ceremonies performed in the sacred sites displace obedience to the Torah and its norms of justice and righteousness, then the worship of God transmogrify into veneration of a Satanic idol and a source of dreadful strife.

The destruction and devastation of Jerusalem, by the Babylonian or the Roman armies, its nostalgic remembrance, and the expectation of its restitution, is the religious and historical matrix of the Bible. The Israeli author Amos Elon has magnificently described how the intense religious feelings evoked by Jerusalem (where the Church of the Holy Sepulcher [or Church of the Resurrection as called by Eastern Christians], the Wailing Wall, the Dome of the Rock, and the Al-Aqsa mosque are located), have transfigured it, in the active imagination of countless believers, pilgrims, holy warriors, and crusaders, into a dangerous, cruel, and bloody city, like perhaps no other in human history.[68] Jews, Christians, and Muslims have

---

68. Elon, *Jerusalem: Battlegrounds of Memory*. See also Armstrong, *Jerusalem: One City, Three Faiths* and Montefiore, *Jerusalem: The Biography*.

claimed that it was there, in old sacred Jerusalem, where Adam and Eve were fashioned at the beginning of biblical times, where the stone for the unfulfilled sacrifice of Isaac by Abraham was located, where Jesus's crucifixion and resurrection took place, and where Muhammad ascended to heaven. In his typical provocative style, James Carroll avers that for "Jews and Christians both, *the destruction of Jerusalem is what . . . defines the heart of our religion.*"[69]

Many Jews, Christians, and Muslims have invoked the famous sorrowful words of the nostalgic biblical hymn to the lost city: "How could we sing the Lord's song in a foreign land? If I forget you, O Jerusalem, let my right hand wither! Let my tongue cling to the roof of my mouth, if I do not remember you, if I do not set Jerusalem above my highest joy" (Psalm 137:4–6). A magnificent lament, indeed! But let us not forget the revengeful last verses of that paean to the sacred city, when the lament is transmuted into vindictive and cruel hatred: "O daughter Babylon, you devastator! Happy shall they be who pay you back what you have done to us! Happy shall they be who take your little ones and dash them against the rock" (Psalm 137:8–9).

Paradoxically, the sacred nature attributed to Jerusalem has been for centuries a reason for extremely violent and sanguinary confrontations. Its sacred sites—the Wailing Wall, remnant of the destroyed second Temple of Yahweh, the Church of the Holy Sepulcher, the Al-Haram Al-Sharif (Noble Sanctuary), enclosing the Dome of the Rock and the Al-Aqsa mosque—places of worship to the divine Spirit, creator and redeemer, have frequently mutated into zones of hatred and warfare. Pilgrims, crusaders and jihadists have arrived at its famous gates "with love in their hearts, the end of the world in their minds, and weapons in their hands."[70] Naomi Shemer's song, "Jerusalem of Gold," composed in the context of the 1967 conquest of East Jerusalem and the old city and which has become sort of a second Israeli national anthem, expresses the outburst of the contemporary nationalistic aspiration of Jerusalem as exclusively a Jewish sacred city.

> Jerusalem of gold, and of light and of bronze,
> I am the lute for all your songs.
> The wells are filled again with water,
> The square with joyous crowd,
> On the Temple Mount within the City,
>
> The shofar rings out loud.

69. Carroll, *Jerusalem, Jerusalem*, 110–11.
70. Ibid., 1.

Pope Urban II's famous and fateful speech at the Council of Clermont (November 27, 1095) is a classic expression of the heinous mixture of the sacred and the sanguinary whenever the matter of contention happens to be Jerusalem. The Pope summons the Frankish knights, so proud of their warring traditions, to rescue Jerusalem, the city honored by the death and resurrection of Christ, from the impure hands of "an accursed race, a race utterly alienated from God."

> Oh, most valiant soldiers ... Enter upon the road to the Holy Sepulchre; wrest that land from the wicked race ... Jerusalem is the navel of the world ... This the Redeemer of the human race has made illustrious by His advent, has beautified by residence, has consecrated by suffering, has redeemed by death, has glorified by burial. This royal city, therefore, situated at the centre of the world, is now held captive by His enemies, and is in subjection to those who do not know God ... She seeks therefore and desires to be liberated, and does not cease to implore you to come to her aid ... Accordingly undertake this journey for the remission of your sins, with the assurance of the imperishable glory of the kingdom of heaven ... It is the will of God![71]

Do we have the spiritual and intellectual resources to reconfigure the debate in such a way that the concepts of "holy city" and "holy land" might become a basis for dialogue, reciprocal respect, understanding and solidarity among the three great Abrahamic monotheistic religions? In the book of *Revelation*, the main core of the eschatological "new heaven and new earth," is a "new Jerusalem, coming down out of heaven from God, prepared as a bride adorned for her husband" (Revelation 21:2). This "new Jerusalem" will become a "home of God among mortals" (Revelation 21:3).[72] Jerusalem, in the biblical apocalyptic perspective, will be the sacred city where the nations, at the end of times, will gather to praise and worship God in peace (Zechariah 8:20—"Many peoples and strong nations shall come to seek the Lord of hosts in Jerusalem, and to entreat the favor of the Lord";

---

71. The citation comes from Robert the Monk's version of Urban II's speech. It can be accessed in http://www.fordham.edu/halsall/source/urban2-5vers.html.

72. Revelation 21:1–4 conveys a reconfiguration of Isaiah 65:17–19: "For I am about to create new heavens and a new earth; the former things shall not be remembered or come to mind. But be glad and rejoice for ever in what I am creating; for I am about to create Jerusalem as a joy, and its people as a delight. I will rejoice in Jerusalem, and delight in my people; no more shall the sound of weeping be heard in it, or the cry of distress."

Isaiah 56:7—"these I will bring to my holy mountain . . . for my house shall be called a house of prayer for all peoples").

As the Palestinian *Kairos* so movingly affirms: "Jerusalem is the heart of our reality. It is, at the same time, symbol of peace and sign of conflict . . . Jerusalem, city of reconciliation, has become a city of discrimination and exclusion, a source of struggle rather than peace."[73] The fate of the diverse peoples inhabiting and sharing Palestine depend, in large part, upon the success or failure of the endeavor to allow peace to prevail upon conflict and strife in Jerusalem. Yehuda Amichai's poem, *If I forget thee, Jerusalem*, faithfully mirrors the nostalgia that many Jews, Muslims, and Christians deeply feel for their beloved holy city:

> If I forget thee, Jerusalem,
> Let my blood be forgotten.
> I shall touch your forehead,
> Forget my own,
> My voice change
> For the second and last time
> To the most terrible of voices —
> Or silence.

PEACE AND RECONCILIATION

Palestinian theology, maybe more emphatically than other liberation theologies, emphasizes the intertwining of justice and reconciliation, truth-telling and forgiveness, prophetic denunciation and peacemaking annunciation, severe critique and hopeful aspiration. The ultimate purpose of the prophetic denunciation is neither the destruction nor the humiliation of the enemy, but the fulfillment of Isaiah's forecast of a new creation, a world free of bellicose violence and devastation, where the conflicting communities, Palestinian and Israeli, Jewish, Christian, and Muslim: "shall build houses and inhabit them; they shall plant vineyards and eat their fruit. They shall not build and another inhabit; they shall not plant and another eat . . . They shall not labor in vain, or bear children for calamity; for they shall be offspring blessed by the Lord—and their descendants as well . . ." (Isaiah 65:21–23). And war will be no more: "they shall beat their swords into plowshares, and their spears into pruning hooks; nation

---

73. *A Moment of Truth: A Word of Faith, Hope, and Love from the Heart of Palestinian Suffering* (Jerusalem, December 15, 2009) 1.1.8.

shall not lift up sword against nation, neither shall they learn war any more" (Isaiah 2:4).

This a dream shared by many Israelis and Palestinians, be they Jews, Muslims, Christians or non-believers. A dream of peace and reconciliation. It is the aspiration of two peoples with severely wounded memories: the memory of the *Shoah* and the memory of the *Al-nakba*.[74] Rightly has Judith Butler highlighted: "Exile may be in fact be a point of departure for thinking about cohabitation. . ."[75] The traumatic and heartrending experience of devastation, persecution, and exile, suffered by both Jews and Palestinians can and should be construed as historical reasons for dialogue rather than conflict. This hopeful aspiration promises to become a main tenet of creative Palestinian theologies.[76] As the Palestinian *Kairos* concludes: "We say that love is possible and mutual trust is possible. Thus, peace is possible and definitive reconciliation also. Thus, justice and security will be attained for all."[77]

Learned readers of Jesus's first public exposition of who he was and what his mission was, according to the Gospel of Luke (4:14–21), easily recognize its intertextual reference to Isaiah 61:1–2.[78] Attention, however, should be paid not only to the concordances between both texts, but also to a significant omission. Jesus concludes his elocution with the proclamation, in his being and deeds, of "the year of the Lord's favor" (Luke 4:19),

---

74. The bibliography on the Shoah is boundless and extremely difficult for any finite individual to master. A recent significant scholarly contribution is Longerich, *Holocaust: The Nazi Persecution and Murder of the Jews*. On the Al-nakba, see Khalidi, ed., *All That Remains*; Pappe, *Ethnic Cleansing of Palestine*. For its background in the Zionist political project prior to 1948, see Masalha, *Expulsion of the Palestinians*.

75. Butler, "Who Owns Kafka?," 3. Butler, a Jewish philosopher, has recently published a severe critique of the policies of the state of Israel regarding the Palestinians, titled *Parting Ways: Jewishness and the Critique of Zionism*, in which she develops her thesis of shared displacement as a possible basis for cohabitation and mutuality.

76. Ateek, *Justice and Only Justice*, chapter 7 ("A Dream of Peace"), 163–75; Raheb, *I Am a Palestinian Christian*, conclusion ("I Have a Dream"), 112–16; Ateek, *Palestinian Christian Cry for Reconciliation*, part III ("The Peace We Dream of"), 153–87.

77. *Moment of Truth*, 9.1.

78. Luke 4:18–19: "The Spirit of the Lord is upon me, because he has anointed me to bring good news to the poor. He has sent me to proclaim release to the captives and recovery of sight to the blind, to let the oppressed go free, to proclaim the year of the Lord's favor." Isaiah 61:1–2: "The spirit of the Lord God is upon me, because the Lord has anointed me; he has sent me to bring good news to the oppressed, to bind up the brokenhearted, to proclaim liberty to the captives, and release to the prisoners; to proclaim the year of the Lord's favor, and the day of vengeance of our God."

a time of liberation of the oppressed and captives, an obvious quotation of Isaiah 61:2a. But he leaves out the prophet's ominous ending—"and the day of vengeance of our God" (61:2b). Jesus's being and mission is therefore liberation *and* reconciliation, not liberation and violent retribution or vengeance.[79]

Certainly, one can find, in many religious canonical scriptures, ominous and sinister images of divine exclusion and sacred violence against those who allegedly contaminate the integrity and purity of religious, national, or ethnic identity. Israeli punitive wars, Christian Crusades, Islamic Jihad, oppressive servitudes, despotic hierarchies, and intolerances of all kinds and types have claimed legitimacy by alluding to sacred texts. They have, too easily, "found justification for savagery in sanctified appeals to the will of God."[80] The idolatry of the "Word of God" has been used to devastate solidarities, consciences, hopes, and human lives.[81] But, those "texts of terror" are neither the decisive nor the predominant ones in most religious myths and symbols. Genuine religious thought, reflecting on the destiny of human history, does not emphasize the sinister symbols of Armageddon and their horsemen of terror, but the hopes for human liberation and universal reconciliation.

In the delicate and sensitive process of dialogue and reconciliation taking place between Israel and Palestine, Christians should be aware of the suffering and pain caused by the not too subtle anti-Semitism ensconced in the way some of the New Testament writings, like the Gospel of John,[82] construe Jesus' fate, intensified by the way those texts have been read and applied during two millennia, in which the Jews were accused of "deicide."[83] However, this deplorable history of Christian Judeophobia should not be a pretext for ignoring the human rights violations of the Palestinian people by the modern state of Israel. Sadly, the West has gone from one kind of anti-Semitism to another, from Judeophobia to Islamophobia. The dreaded "other" is not any more the Jew, but the Muslim. Either kind of phobic depreciation is a nefarious obstacle in the project of achieving peace with

---

79. See Bosch, *Transforming Mission*, 108–13.

80. Carroll, *Jerusalem, Jerusalem*, 164–65.

81. See Schwartz, *Curse of Cain*; Armstrong, *Battle for God*; Juergensmeyer, *Terror in the Mind of God*; and Ali, *Clash of Fundamentalisms*.

82. Pagels, *Origin of Satan*.

83. See for example, John Chrysostom, *Discourses against Judaizing Christians*. On this lamentable issue of Christian anti-Semitism and its biblical and theological sources, see Ruether, *Faith and Fratricide: The Theological Roots of Anti-Semitism*.

justice. It performs its dehumanization by avoiding the recognition of the rich and complex diversities of the demonized race, ethnic, national, or religious "other."[84]

That project of reconciliation and righteousness has been difficult and, to say the least, tortuous. It requires, today more than ever before, intellectual understanding and ethical empathy regarding the wave of anti-Judaism that between the Dreyfus affair and the *Shoah* rendered unsuccessful the sophisticate attempts by the Diaspora Jews to achieve emancipation and assimilation into European culture. But it also requires similar intellectual understanding and ethical empathy of the sufferings of the Palestinian people caused by the *Yishuv*,[85] its Zionist nationalistic ideology, and its military actions that led to a merciless ethnic cleansing. The first were victims of the infamous "final solution," the genocidal culmination of centuries of exclusion and persecution, perpetrated by heirs of the Christian Western civilization, memorialized in the sad and sober elegance of Yad Vashem. The second are the sufferers of the wrath and vindictiveness of the children of Yahweh, their return to Zion and their reliance in the kind of strong-armed attitude once expressed in the hard to read words by Moshe Dayan, the renowned Israeli military strategist, "our life's choice—to be prepared and armed, strong and tough, lest our fist would lose grip of the sword and our life would cease."[86]

As Miroslav Volf, with his characteristic lucidity, has emphasized, in a telling and critical conversation with Elie Wiesel, wounded memories do not necessarily lead to exclusion. They may, contrariwise, become a shared source for the humanly dignifying act of reciprocal recognition and embrace.[87] What Sigmund Freud, in *Moses and Monotheism*, claims as a distinctive peculiarity of the Jewish people, namely that "they defy oppression, that even the most cruel persecutions have not succeeded in

---

84. The contemporary meaningful pluralities within Islamic culture are disclosed in the books of Anouar Majid, *Unveiling Traditions: Postcolonial Islam in a Polycentric World*; *Freedom and Orthodoxy: Islam and Difference in the Post-Andalusian Age*; and *Call for Heresy: Why Dissent Is Vital to Islam and America*.

85. *Yishuv* is the Hebrew term for the Jewish community in Palestine prior to the declaration of the state of Israel, including the pre-Zionist era (Old *Yishuv*) as well as the Zionists of the late Ottoman Turkish rule and British mandate eras (New *Yishuv*).

86. Quoted by Piterberg, *Returns of Zionism*, 193.

87. Volf, *Exclusion and Embrace*. Born in Croatia, Volf experienced the painful and violent fragmentation of the former Yugoslavia, torn apart, among other things, by the different wounded memories and religiosities of the Serbian, Croatian, and Bosnian nations.

exterminating them,"[88] can be similarly predicated of the Palestinian people.[89] Both national communities have faced oppression and persecution; both carry a painful fissure at the heart of their collective identity; both face the sometimes attractive temptation to indulge in a rigid path of coercive and coercing exclusionary identity; both also resolutely hope and pray for peace and reconciliation.

Edward Said, in an article published less than a year before his demise, emphasized the requirement to avoid exclusionary attitudes vis-à-vis the "others": "Purifying the land of 'aliens,' whether it is spoken of by Muslims, Christians or Jews, is a defilement of human life as it is lived by billions of people who are mixed by race, history, ethnic identity, religion or nationality."[90] Jonathan Sacks, Chief Rabbi of the United Hebrew Congregations in the United Kingdom, who as a Jew confesses that he carries deep within himself "the tears and sufferings of my grandparents and theirs through the generations," and that "the story of my people is a narrative of centuries of exiles and expulsions, persecutions and pogroms," admonishes Israelis not to convert that history into a justifying narrative of violence and injustice against the Palestinians. "Until Israelis and Palestinians are able to listen to one another, hear each other's anguish and anger and make cognitive space for one another's hopes, there is no way forward."[91]

The sacred vision of liberation *and* reconciliation, foreseen in the hallowed scriptures of the three great monotheistic Semitic religions, requires from Israeli and Palestinian civic and religious leaders rigorous critical consciousness and the disposition to pay the price that such an attribute frequently entails.[92] This dream of deliverance and peace, so meaningful

---

88. Freud, *Moses and Monotheism*, 146.

89. See Said, *Freud and the Non-European*.

90. Edward Said, "Real Change Means *People* Must Change: Immediate Imperatives," *CounterPunch*, December 21, 2002. Accessed in http://www.counterpunch.org/said1221.html.

91. Sacks, *Dignity of Difference*, 189–90. On this subject, it is also to be welcomed the recent book by the Jewish-American Rabbi, Michael Lerner, *Embracing Israel/Palestine*.

92. For a vivid example of the hardships that such a rigorous critical consciousness might entail for the intellectual who dares to embody it, see Ilan Pappe's memoir, *Out of Frame: The Struggle for Academic Freedom in Israel*. His life and academic work is an outstanding example of rigorous critical consciousness, a living rejection of the nationalistic principle attributed to another scholar/politician of a similarly small nation surrounded by enemies, the Croatian Franjo Tudjman, who once said to a colleague and compatriot: "Of course one should write the truth, but only when it is not contrary to the national interest." Quoted by Goldstein, "Turning Point for Croatia," 61. Another

for Israeli and Palestinian Christians, Muslims, and Jews, is also shared by many of us, *goyim* who in Gentile lands hope and pray that the time might come when in Palestine "justice and peace kiss each other" (Ps 85:10).[93]

> Stripped of my name and identity?
> On a soil I nourished with my own hands?
> Today Job cried out
> Filling the sky:
> Don't make an example of me again!
> Oh, gentlemen, Prophets,
> Don't ask the trees for their names
> Don't ask the valleys who their mother is
> From my forehead bursts the sword of light
> And from my hand springs the water of the river
> All the hearts of the people are my identity
> So take away my passport!
>
> —Mahmoud Darwish

---

committed intellectual, who displayed constantly a rigorous critical consciousness regarding the mistakes, flaws, and misdoings, in his case of the Palestinian leadership, was Edward Said. See the fine eulogy of Said by Nur Masalha, "Cultural Resistance and the Secular Humanist Challenge: Edward W. Said, Zionism and Rethinking the Question of Palestine," in Masalha, *Bible and Zionism*, 279–309.

93. See Rivera-Pagán, "Desafíos teológicos del conflicto palestino-israelí," 6–9; "Religion, War and Peace: Towards an Emancipatory Palestinian Theology," 169–88; and "Toward an Emancipatory Palestinian Theology: Hermeneutical Paradigms and Horizons," 89–117, 399–408.

Bibliography

Abellán, José Luis. "Los orígenes españoles del mito del 'buen salvaje.' Fray Bartolomé de Las Casas y su antropología utópica." *Revista de Indias* 36:145–46 (1976) 157–79.
Achebe, Chinua. *Home and Exile*. New York: Anchor, 2000.
———. *Things Fall Apart*. New York: Fawcett Crest, 1959.
Acosta, José de. *De procuranda indorum salute*. Translated and edited by G. Stewart McIntosh. 2 vols. Tayport, Scotland: Mac Research, 1996.
Akenson, Donald Harman. *God's Peoples: Covenant and Land in South Africa, Israel, and Ulster*. Ithaca: Cornell University Press, 1992.
Ali, Tariq. *The Clash of Fundamentalisms: Crusades, Jihads and Modernity*. London: Verso, 2002.
Althaus-Reid, Marcella. *Indecent Theology: Theological Perversions in Sex, Gender and Politics*. London: Routledge, 2000.
———. *The Queer God*. London: Routledge, 2003.
———. "El Tocado (Le Toucher): Sexual Irregularities in the Translation of God (the Word) in Jesus." In *Derrida and Religion: Other Testaments*, edited by Yvonne Sherwood and Kevin Hart, 393–406. New York: Routledge, 2004.
Atwood, Margaret. *The Handmaid's Tale*. New York: Knopf, 2006.
Alves, Rubem. *A Theology of Human Hope*. Washington, DC: Corpus, 1969.
———. "Towards a Theology of Liberation: An Exploration of the Encounter Between the Languages of Humanistic Messianism and Messianic Humanism." PhD diss., Princeton Theological Seminary, 1968.
André-Vincent, Ph. I. "Le prophétisme de Barthélemy de Las Casas." *Nouvelle revue théologique* 101 (1979) 541–60.
Anzaldúa, Gloria. *Borderlands/La Frontera: The New Mestiza*. San Francisco: Aunt Lute, 1999.
Arenal, Celestino del. "La teoría de la servidumbre natural en el pensamiento español de los siglos XVI y XVII." *Historiografía y bibliografía americanistas* 19–20 (1975–76) 67–124.
Arens, W. *The Man-Eating Myth: Anthropology and Anthropophagy*. New York: Oxford University Press, 1979.
Arguedas, José María. *The Fox from Up Above and the Fox from Down Below*. Translated by Frances Horning Barraclough. Pittsburgh: University of Pittsburgh Press, 2000.
———. *El zorro de arriba y el zorro de abajo*. 1969. Reprint, Madrid: Consejo Superior de Investigaciones Científicas, 1990.

Bibliography

Aristophanes. "Lysistrata." In *The Complete Greek Drama*, edited by Whitney J. Oates and Eugene O'Neill Jr., 2:803–860. New York: Random House, 1938.

Aristotle. "Politics." In *The Basic Works of Aristotle*, edited and with an introduction by Richard McKeon, 1113–1316. New York: Random House, 1941.

Armstrong, Karen. *The Battle for God*. New York: Knopf, 2000.

———. *Jerusalem: One City, Three Faiths*. New York: Ballantine, 1996.

Ashcroft, Bill, Gareth Griffiths, and Helen Tiffin. *Post-Colonial Studies: The Key Concepts*. London: Routledge, 1998.

Assmann, Hugo. *Opresión–Liberación: Desafío a los cristianos*. Montevideo: Tierra Nueva, 1971.

Ateek, Naim Stifan. *Justice and Only Justice: A Palestinian Theology of Liberation*. Maryknoll, NY: Orbis, 1989.

———. *A Palestinian Christian Cry for Reconciliation*. Maryknoll, NY: Orbis, 2008.

Bakhtin, Mikhail. *The Dialogic Imagination: Four Essays*. Austin: University of Texas Press, 1981.

Balderrama, Francisco, and Raymond Rodríguez. *Decade of Betrayal: Mexican Repatriation in the 1930s*. Albuquerque: University of New Mexico Press, 2006.

Baldwin, James. *Notes of a Native Son*. Boston: Beacon, 1955.

Bales, Kevin. *Disposable People: New Slavery in the Global Economy*. Berkeley, CA: University of California Press, 2004.

Barkan, Elazar, and Marie-Denise Shelton, eds. *Borders, Exiles, Diasporas*. Stanford: Stanford University Press, 1998.

Bataillon, Marcel. *Erasme et l'Espagne*. Genève: Librairie Droz, 1991, orig. 1937.

———. *Études sur Bartolomé de las Casas*. Paris: Centre de Recherches de l'Institut d'Études Hispaniques, 1966.

———. "Novo mundo e fim do mundo." *Revista de historia* (São Paulo) 18 (1954) 343–51.

Bauman, Zygmunt. *Postmodernity and Its Discontents*. Cambridge: Polity, 1997.

———. *Wasted Lives: Modernity and Its Outcasts*. Cambridge: Polity, 2004.

Benedict XVI. *Caritas in Veritate*. San Francisco, CA: Ignatius, 2009.

Benenisti, Meron. *Sacred Landscape: The Buried History of the Holy Land Since 1948*. Berkeley: The University of California Press, 2000.

Benfey, Christopher. "A Tale of Two Iliads." *The New York Review of Books*, September 25, 2003, 82.

Bhabha, Homi. *The Location of Culture*. London and New York: Routledge, 2001.

Biermann, Benno. "Das Requerimiento in der spanischen Conquista." *Neue Zeitschrift für Missionswissenschaft* 6 (1950) 94–114.

Blázquez Ruiz, Francisco Javier. "Derechos humanos, inmigración, integración." In *Ciudadanía, multiculturalidad e inmigración*, edited by José A. Zamora, 73–133. Navarra, España: Editorial Verbo Divino, 2003.

Bloch, Ernst. *Atheismus im Christentum*. Frankfurt am Main: Suhrkamp, 1968.

Blount, Brian K. *Can I Get a Witness? Reading Revelation Through African American Culture*. Louisville: Westminster John Knox, 2005.

Bock, Kim Yong, ed. *Minjung Theology: People as the Subjects of History*. Singapore: Commission on Theological Concerns, Christian Conference of Asia, 1981.

Boer, Roland, editor. *Postcolonialism and the Hebrew Bible: The Next Step*. Atlanta: Society of Biblical Literature, 2013.

Boff, Leonardo. *Eclesiogênese: as comunidades eclesiais de base reinventam a Igreja*. Petrópolis: Vozes, 1977.

———. *Igreja, carisma e poder: ensaios de eclesiologia militante*. Petrópolis, Brazil: Vozes, 1981.

———. *Jesus Cristo libertador; ensaio de cristologia crítica para o nosso tempo*. Petrópolis: Vozes, 1972.

———. *Teología desde el cautiverio*. Bogotá: Indo-American Press Service, 1975.

Bonhöffer, Dietrich. *Letters and Papers from Prison*. Edited by Eberhard Bethge. London: Folio Society, 2000.

Borges, Jorge Luis. *This Craft of Verse*. Cambridge, MA: Harvard University Press, 2000.

Bosch, David J. *Transforming Mission: Paradigm Shifts in Theology of Mission*. Maryknoll, NY: Orbis, 2002.

Boulding, Elise. *Cultures of Peace: The Hidden Side of History*. Syracuse, NY: Syracuse University Press, 2000.

———. "Feminist Inventions in the Art of Peacemaking: A Century Overview." *Peace & Change*, 20, No. 4 (1995) 408–38.

Bowe, John. *Nobodies: Modern American Slave Labor and the Dark Side of the New Global Economy*. New York: Random House, 2007.

Brady, Robert L. "The Role of Las Casas in the Emergence of Negro Slavery in the New World." *Revista de Historia de América* 61–62 (1966) 43–55.

Brueggemann, Walter. *The Land: Place as Gift, Promise, and Challenge in Biblical Faith*. Minneapolis: Fortress, 2002.

Buchanan, Patrick J. *State of Emergency: The Third World Invasion and Conquest of America*. New York: Thomas Dunne /St. Martin's, 2008.

Butler, Judith. *Parting Ways: Jewishness and the Critique of Zionism*. New York: Columbia University Press, 2012.

———. "Who Owns Kafka?" *The London Review of Books* 33.5 (3 March 2011).

Camus, Albert. *Le mythe de Sisyphe: essai sur l'absurde*. Paris: Gallimard, 1942.

Cantú, Francesca. "Evoluzione e significato della dottrina della restituzione in Bartolomé de las Casas." *Critica storica* (Rome) 12.2–4 (1975) 55–143, 231–319.

Capdevila, Nestor. *Las Casas, une politique de l'humanité: L'homme et l'empire de la foi*. Paris: Cerf, 1998.

Carpentier, Alejo. *El arpa y la sombra*. México, DF: Siglo XXI, 1979.

Carroll, James. *Jerusalem, Jerusalem: How the Ancient City Ignited Our Modern World*. Boston/New York: Houghton Mifflin Harcourt, 2011.

Carroll R., M. Daniel. *Christians at the Border: Immigration, the Church, and the Bible*. Grand Rapids: Michigan: Baker, 2008.

Carson, Clayborne, and Kris Shepard, eds. *A Call to Conscience: The Landmark Speeches of Dr. Martin Luther King, Jr.* New York: Warner, 2001.

Castillo Guerra, Jorge E. "A Theology of Migration: Toward an Intercultural Methodology." In *A Promised Land, A Perilous Journey: Theological Perspectives on Migration*, edited by Daniel G. Groody and Gioacchino Campese, 243–70. Notre Dame, IN: University of Notre Dame Press, 2008.

Castles, Stephen and Mark J. Miller. *The Age of Migration: International Population Movements in the Modern World*. 4th ed. revised and updated. New York: Guilford, 2009.

Cervantes Gabarrón, José. "El inmigrante en las tradiciones bíblicas." En *Ciudadanía, multiculturalidad e inmigración*, edited by José A. Zamora, 241–88. Navarra, Spain: Verbo Divino, 2003.

Bibliography

Cervantes-Ortiz, Leopoldo. *Serie de sueños: la teología ludo-erótico-poética de Rubem Alves*. Quito, Ecuador: Consejo Latinoamericano de Iglesias, 2003.

Chasteen, John Charles. *Born in Blood and Fire: A Concise History of Latin America*. New York: Norton, 2001.

Chrysostom, John. *Discourses against Judaizing Christians*. Washington, DC: Catholic University of America Press, 1979.

Clarke, Sathianathan. *Dalits and Christianity: Subaltern Religion and Liberation Theology in India*. Delhi: Oxford University Press, 1998.

Cliff, Michelle. *No Telephone to Heaven*. New York: Plume, 1996, orig. 1987.

Cobban, Helena. *The Palestinian Liberation Organisation: People, Power and Politics*. Cambridge: Cambridge University Press, 1984.

Coleridge, Samuel Taylor. *The Complete Poetical Works*. Oxford: Clarendon, 1912.

Coles, Robert. *Simone Weil: A Modern Pilgrimage*. Woodstock, Vermont: Skylight Paths, 2001.

Colón, Cristóbal. "Carta a Luis de Santángel." En *Textos y documentos completos*, editado por Consuelo Varela, y *Nuevas cartas*, edited by Juan Gil, 219–26. Madrid: Alianza Editorial, 1995.

———. *Textos y documentos completos*. Edited by Consuelo Varela and *Nuevas cartas*, edited by Juan Gil. Madrid: Alianza, 1995.

Columbus, Christopher. *A New and Fresh English Translation of the Letter of Columbus Announcing the Discovery of America*. Translated and edited by Samuel Eliot Morison. Madrid: Gráficas Yagües, 1959.

Cone, James. *Black Theology & Black Power*. New York: Seabury, 1969.

———. *A Black Theology of Liberation*. Philadelphia, Lippincott, 1970.

———. *The Spirituals and Blues*. New York: Seabury, 1972.

Cook Steicke, Elisabeth. *La mujer como extranjera en Israel: Estudio exegético de Esdras 9–10*. San José, Costa Rica: SEBILA, 2011.

Cortés, Hernán *Documentos cortesianos, 1518–1528*. Edited by José Luis Martínez. México, DF: Universidad Nacional Autónoma de México/Fondo de Cultura Económica, 1990.

———. *Letters from Mexico (1520–6)*. Translated and edited by Anthony R. Pagden. Oxford: Oxford University Press, 1972.

Courtine-Denamy, Sylvie. *Three Women in Dark Times: Edith Stein, Hannah Arendt, Simone Weil*. Ithaca, NY: Cornell University Press, 2000.

Croatto, José Severino. *Exodus, a Hermeneutics of Freedom*. Maryknoll, NY: Orbis, 1981.

Dabashi, Hamid. *Islamic Liberation Theology: Resisting the Empire*. London and New York: Routledge, 2008.

Danner, Mark. *Torture and Truth: America, Abu Ghraib, and the War on Terror*. New York: New York Review of Books, 2004.

Darwish, Mahmoud. *Journal of an Ordinary Grief*. Brooklyn, NY: Archipelago, 2010.

———. *Unfortunately, It Was Paradise*. Berkeley: University of California Press, 2003.

Davenport, Frances Gardiner, ed. *European Treaties Bearing on the History of the United States and Its Dependencies to 1648*. Washington, DC: Carnegie Institution of Washington, 1917.

Davis, David Brion. *The Problem of Slavery in Western Culture*. Ithaca: Cornell University Press, 1961.

Díaz-Quiñones, Arcadio. *El arte de bregar: ensayos*. San Juan: Ediciones Callejón, 2000.

Dobbs-Allsopp, F. W. *Lamentations*. Louisville: Westminster John Knox, 2002.

Dorfman, Ariel. *Death and the Maiden*. New York: Penguin, 1992.
Dube, Musa W. *Postcolonial Feminist Interpretation of the Bible*. St. Louis: Chalice, 2000.
Dunn, Oliver, and James Kelley, Jr., *The Diario of Christopher Columbus's First Voyage to America, 1492–1493. Abstracted by Bartolomé de las Casas*. Transcribed and translated into English, with notes and a concordance of the Spanish. Norman and London: University of Oklahoma Press, 1989.
Dussel, Enrique. *1492: El encubrimiento del otro (Hacia el origen del "mito de la modernidad")*. Bogotá: Ediciones, 1992.
———. *Les évêques hispano-américains: défenseurs et évangélisateurs de l'indien (1504–1620)*. Wiesbaden: Franz Steiner, 1970.
———. *Invention of the Americas: Eclipse of "the Other" & the Myth of Modernity*. New York: Continuum, 1995.
———. *Política de la liberación. Historia mundial y crítica*. Madrid: Editorial Trotta, 2007.
Duverger, Christian. *La Conversion des Indiens de Nouvelle-Espagne avec le texte des "Colloques des douze" de Bernardino de Sahagún (1564)*. Paris: Seuil, 1987.
Duviols, Pierre. *La lutte contre les religions autochtones dans le Pérou colonial: l'extirpation de l'idolatrie entre 1532 et 1660*. París-Lima: Institut Français d'Études Andines, 1971.
Ebadi, Shirin. *History and documentation of human rights in Iran*. New York: Bibliotheca Persica, 2000.
Ehrenreich, Ben. "A Lucrative War." *The New York Review of Books* 32.20 (21 October 2010) 15–18.
Eliot, Thomas Stearns. "Murder in the Cathedral." In *The Complete Poems and Plays, 1909–1950*, 173–221. New York: Harcourt, Brace & Company, 1958.
Ellacuría, Ignacio, and Jon Sobrino, eds. *Mysterium liberationis: Conceptos fundamentales de la Teología de la Liberación*. Madrid: Trotta, 1990.
Ellis, Marc H. *Toward a Jewish Theology of Liberation*. Waco, TX: Baylor University Press, 2004.
Elon, Amos. *Jerusalem: Battlegrounds of Memory*. New York: Kodansha International, 1995.
Erskine, Noel Leo. *Decolonizing Theology: A Caribbean Perspective*. Trenton, NJ: Africa World, 1998.
Euripides. "Andromache." In *The Complete Greek Drama*, edited by Whitney J. Oates and Eugene O'Neill Jr., 2:843–78. New York: Random House, 1938.
———. "Hecuba." In *The Complete Greek Drama*, edited by Whitney J. Oates and Eugene O'Neill Jr., 1:803–40. New York: Random House, 1938.
———. "Hecuba." In *Electra and Other Plays*, translated by E. P. Coleridge, 24–42. New York: Digireads, 2009.
———. "The Women of Troy." In *The Bacchae and Other Plays*, 89–133. London: Penguin, 1973.
European Commission. "Roma in Europe: The Implementation of European Union Instruments and Policies for Roma Inclusion (Progress Report 2008–2010)." Brussels, April 7, 2010 SEC (2010) 400 final.
Eusebius of Caesarea. *Ecclesiastical History*. Cambridge, MA: Harvard University Press, 1998.
Falcón, Angelo. *Atlas of Stateside Puerto Ricans*. Washington, DC: Puerto Rico Federal Affairs Administration, 2004.
Fanon, Franz. *Peau Noir, Masques Blancs*. Paris: Seuil, 1952.
———. *The Wretched of the Earth*. New York: Grove, 1968.

Bibliography

Finkelstein, Israel, and Neil Asher Silberman. *The Bible Unearthed: Archaeology's New Vision of Ancient Israel and the Origin of its Sacred Texts*. New York: Free, 2002.

Fitzgerald, Frances. *Fire in the Lake: The Vietnamese and the Americans in Vietnam*. Boston: Little, Brown, 1972.

Flannery, Austin P., ed. *Vatican Council II. The Basic Sixteen Documents: Constitutions, Decrees, Declarations*. Northport, NY: Costello, 1996.

Fornet-Betancourt, Raúl, ed. *Migration and Interculturality: Theological and Philosophical Challenges*. Aachen, Germany: Missionswissenschaftliches Institut Missio e.V., 2004.

Fraser, Nancy, and Axel Honneth. *Redistribution or Recognition? A Political-Philosophical Exchange*. London: Verso, 2003.

Fredrickson, George M. *Diverse Nations: Explorations in the History of Racial & Ethnic Pluralism*. Boulder, CO: Paradigm, 2006.

Freire, Paulo. *Educação como prática da liberdade*. Rio de Janeiro: Paz e Terra, 1967.

———. *Pedagogía del oprimido*. Montevideo: Tierra Nueva, 1970.

Freud, Sigmund. *Moses and Monotheism*. Letchworth, Hertfordshire, UK: Hogarth and the Institute of Psycho-analysis, 1939, orig. 1937.

———. *Totem and Taboo: Resemblances Between the Psychic Lives of Savages and Neurotics*. New York: Random House, 1946, orig, 1913.

Friede, Juan. *Bartolomé de Las Casas: precursor del anticolonialismo*. México, DF: Siglo XXI, 1974.

Fukuyama, Francis. *The End of History and the Last Man*. New York: Free, 1992.

García Icazbalceta, Joaquín. *Colección de documentos para la historia de México*. Nendeln, Liechtenstein: Kraus Reprint, 1971.

García, Rubén. *La conversion a los indios de Bartolomé de las Casas*. Buenos Aires: Don Bosco, 1987.

García Martínez, Alfonso, ed. *Libro rojo/Tratado de París: Documentos presentados a las cortes en la legislatura de 1898 por el ministro de Estado*. Río Piedras, Puerto Rico: Editorial de la Universidad de Puerto Rico, 1988.

Gichaara, Jonathan. "Issues in African Liberation Theology." *Black Theology: An International Journal*, 3, No. 1 (2005) 75–85.

Giménez Fernández, Manuel. "Algo más sobre las bulas alejandrinas de 1493 referentes a las Indias." *Anales de la Universidad Hispalense* (Sevilla) 8.3 (1945) 37–86; 9.1, 115–26.

———. *Bartolomé de las Casas, Vol. I: Delegado de Cisneros para la reformación de las Indias*. Sevilla: Escuela de Estudios Hispanoamericanos, 1953.

———. *Bartolomé de las Casas, Vol. II: Capellán de Carlos I, poblador de Cumaná*. Sevilla: Escuela de Estudios Hispanoamericanos, 1960.

———. *Nuevas consideraciones sobre la historia, sentido y valor de las bulas alejandrinas de 1493 referentes a las Indias*. Sevilla: Escuela de Estudios Hispano-Americanos de la Universidad de Sevilla, 1944.

Goldstein, Slavko "A Turning Point for Croatia." *The New York Review of Books* 58.11 (June 23, 2011) 61.

Gonzalez Dávila, Gil. *Teatro eclesiástico de la primitiva iglesia de la Nueva España en las Indias Occidentales* (1649). Madrid: José Porrúa Turanzas, 1959.

Goodspeed, Edgar J. "The Address to Diognetus." In *The Apostolic Fathers: An American Translation*, 273–84. New York: Harper, 1950.

Gottwald, Norman K., ed. *The Bible and Liberation: Political and Social Hermeneutics*. Maryknoll, NY: Orbis, 1983.

Greenblatt, Stephen. *Marvelous Possessions*. Chicago: University of Chicago Press, 1992.
Greene, Graham. *The Power and the Glory*. London: Penguin, 1990, orig. 1940.
Greider, Brett. "Crossing Deep Rivers: The Liberation Theology of Gustavo Gutiérrez in the Light of the Narrative Poetics of José María Arguedas." PhD diss., Graduate Theological Union, 1988.
Griffin, Nigel, editor. *Repertorium Columbianum, Las Casas on Columbus: Background and the Second and Fourth Voyage*. Introduction by Anthony Pagden. Turnhout, Belgium: Brepols, 1999.
Groody, Daniel G., and Gioacchino Campese, eds. *A Promised Land, A Perilous Journey: Theological Perspectives on Migration*. Notre Dame, IN: University of Notre Dame Press, 2008.
Gutiérrez de Arce, Manuel. "Regio patronato indiano (Ensayo de valoración histórico-canónica)." *Anuario de estudios americanos*, 11 (1954) 107–68.
Gutiérrez, Gustavo. *Las Casas: In Search of the Poor of Jesus Christ*. Maryknoll, NY: Orbis, 1993.
———. "Las Casas y Paulo III." *Páginas* (Lima) 16.107 (February 1991) 33–42.
———. *The Density of the Present: Selected Writings*. Maryknoll, N Y: Orbis, 1999.
———. "The Meaning and Scope of Medellín." In *The Density of the Present: Selected Writings*, 59–101. Maryknoll, NY: Orbis, 1999.
———. *Teología de la liberación: perspectivas*. Salamanca: Sígueme, 1973.
———. *A Theology of Liberation*. Maryknoll, NY: Orbis, 1988.
Hanke, Lewis U. *All Mankind is One: A Study of the Disputation between Bartolomé de Las Casas and Juan Ginés de Sepúlveda in 1550 on the Intellectual and Religious Capacity of the American Indians*. DeKalb: Northern Illinois University Press, 1974.
———. *Aristotle and the American Indians: A Study in Race Prejudice in the Modern World*. Chicago: Henry Regnery, 1959.
———. "Pope Paul III and the American Indians." *Harvard Theological Review* 30 (1937) 56–102.
———. *The Spanish Struggle for Justice in the Conquest of America*. Philadelphia: University of Pennsylvania Press, 1949.
Harding, Jeremy. "The Deaths Map." *London Review of Books* 33.20 (20 October 2011) 7–13.
Hardt, Michael, and Antonio Negri. *Multitude: War and Democracy in the Age of Empire*. New York: Penguin, 2004.
Hennelly, Alfred T. *Liberation Theology: A Documentary History*. Maryknoll, NY: Orbis, 1992.
Hera, Alberto de la. "El derecho de los indios a la libertad y a la fe: la bula *Sublimis Deus* y los problemas indianos que la motivaron." *Anuario de historia del derecho español*, 26 (1956) 89–182.
———. "El Patronato y el Vicariato Regio en Indias." In *Historia de la Iglesia en Hispanoamérica y Filipinas* (xv–xix centuries), under direction of Pedro Borges, 1:63–79. Madrid: Biblioteca de Autores Cristianos, 1992.
———. "El regalismo indiano." En *Historia de la Iglesia en Hispanoamérica y Filipinas* (xv–xix centuries), under direction of Pedro Borges, 1:81–97. Madrid: Biblioteca de Autores Cristianos, 1992.
Hernáez, Francisco Javier. *Colección de bulas, breves y otros documentos relativos a la iglesia de América y Filipinas*. Vaduz: Klaus Reprint, 1964, orig. 1879.

Bibliography

Higham, John. *Strangers in the Land: Patterns of American Nativism, 1860–1925.* New York: Atheneum, 1968.

Hinkelammert, Franz. *El grito del sujeto: del teatro-mundo del evangelio de Juan al perro-mundo de la globalización.* San José, Costa Rica: DEI, 1998.

Hobsbawm, Eric J. *The Age of Empire, 1875–1914.* New York: Pantheon, 1987.

———. *Age of Extremes: The Short Twentieth Century, 1914–1991.* London: Michael Joseph, 1994.

Hoffman, Abraham. *Unwanted Mexican Americans in the Great Depression: Repatriation Pressures, 1929–1939.* Tucson: University of Arizona Press, 1974.

Horne, Alistair. *A Savage War of Peace: Algeria 1954–1962.* New York: Penguin, 1987.

Horsley, Richard A. *Jesus and Empire: the Kingdom of God and the New World Disorder.* Minneapolis: Fortress, 2003.

———. *Paul and Empire: Religion and Power in Roman Imperial Society.* Harrisburg, PA: Trinity Press International, 1997.

———. *Paul and the Roman Imperial Order.* Harrisburg, PA: Trinity Press International, 2004.

———, ed. *In the Shadow of Empire: Reclaiming the Bible as a History of Faithful Resistance.* Louisville, KY: Westminster John Knox, 2008.

Houston, Walter J. *Contending for Justice: Ideologies and Theologies of Social Justice in the Old Testament.* London: T. & T. Clark, 2006.

Hume, David. *The Natural History of Religion.* London: A. & C. Black, 1956.

Huntington, Samuel P. "The Clash of Civilizations?" *Foreign Affairs* 72.3 (Summer 1993) 22–49.

———. *The Clash of Civilizations and the Remaking of World Order.* New York: Simon & Schuster, 1996.

———. "The Hispanic Challenge." *Foreign Policy* (March/April 2004) 30–45.

———. *Who Are We? The Challenges to America's National Identity.* New York: Simon & Schuster, 2004.

Irvin, Dale. "The Church, the Urban and the Global: Mission in an Age of Global Cities." *International Bulletin of Missionary Research"* 33.4 (October 2009) 177–82.

Joh, Wonhee Anne. *Heart of the Cross: a Postcolonial Christology.* Louisville: Westminster John Knox, 2006.

Jordan, Mark D. *The Invention of Sodomy in Christian Theology.* Chicago: The University of Chicago Press, 1997.

Joyce, James. *Ulysses.* New York: Random House, 1946, orig. 1914.

Juergensmeyer, Mark. *Terror in the Mind of God: The Global Rise of Religious Violence.* Berkeley and Los Angeles: University of California Press, 2000.

Kanstroom, Daniel. *Deportation Nation: Outsiders in American History.* Cambridge, MA: Harvard University Press, 2007.

Keller, Catherine. *God and Power: Counter-Apocalyptic Journeys.* Minneapolis: Fortress, 2005.

Keller, Catherine, Michael Nausner, and Mayra Rivera, eds. *Postcolonial Theologies: Divinity and Empire.* St. Louis: Chalice, 2004.

Khader, Jamal, and Angela Hawash-Abu Eita, eds. *Violence, Non-Violence and Religion* (Third International Conference on Christian-Muslim Relations). Bethlehem: Bethlehem University, Department of Religious Studies, 2011.

Khalidi, Walid, ed. *All That Remains: The Palestinian Villages Occupied and Depopulated by Israel in 1948.* Washington, DC: Institute for Palestine Studies, 2006.

Kremer, Roberta S., ed. *Memory and Mastery: Primo Levi as Writer and Witness.* Albany: State University of New York Press, 2001.
Krüger, René. *La diáspora: De experiencia traumática a paradigma eclesiológico.* Buenos Aires: ISEDET, 2008.
Kwok, Pui-lan. *Postcolonial Imagination and Feminist Theology.* Louisville, KY: Westminster John Knox, 2005.
Kwok, Pui-lan, Don H. Compier, and Joerg Rieger, editors. *Empire: The Christian Tradition. New Readings of Classical Theologians.* Minneapolis, MN: Fortress, 2007.
Laclau, Ernesto and Chantal Mouffe. *Hegemony and Socialist Strategy: Toward a Radical Democratic Politics* (2nd. ed.). London: Verso, 2001.
Las Casas, Bartolomé de. *Brevísima relación de la destrucción de Africa: Preludio de la destrucción de Indias. Primera defensa de los guanches y negros contra su esclavización.* Edición y notas por Isacio Pérez Fernández, O. P. Salamanca-Lima: Editorial San Esteban-Instituto Bartolomé de las Casas, 1989.
———. *In Defense of the Indians.* Translated by Stafford Poole, C. M. DeKalb: Northern Illinois University Press, 1992.
———. *Historia de las Indias.* In Bartolomé de Las Casas. *Obras completas.* Madrid: Alianza Editorial, 1988–1998, Vols. 3–5.
———. *History of the Indies.* Translated and edited by André Collard. New York: Harper, 1971.
———. *Obras completas* (14 volúmenes). Madrid: Alianza Editorial, 1988–1998.
———. *The Only Way.* Edited by Helen Rand Parish and translated by Francis Patrick Sullivan, S. J. New York: Paulist, 1992.
———. *De regia potestate o derecho de autodeterminación.* Edited by Luciano Pereña et al. Corpus Hispanorum de Pace 8. Madrid: Consejo Superior de Investigaciones Científicas, 1969.
———. *Del único modo de atraer a todos los pueblos a la verdadera religión.* México, D. F.: Fondo de Cultura Económica, 1942.
Leonhardt, David. "Truth, Fiction, and Lou Dobbs." *The New York Times* (May 30 2007) C1.
Lerner, Michael. *Embracing Israel/Palestine: A Strategy to Heal and Transform the Middle East.* Berkeley, CA: North Atlantic, 2012.
Leturia, Pedro de, S. I. *Relaciones entre la Santa Sede e Hispanoamérica, Vol. I: Época del Real Patronato, 1493–1800.* Caracas: Sociedad Bolivariana de Venezuela, 1959.
Libânio João B. e Maria Clara L. Bingemer. *Escatologia Cristã: O Novo Céu e a Nova Terra.* Petrópolis, Brasil: Vozes, 1985.
Longerich, Peter. *Holocaust: The Nazi Persecution and Murder of the Jews.* Oxford: Oxford University Press, 2010.
López de Gómara, Francisco. *Historia general de las indias* (1552). Madrid: Espasa-Calpe, 1941.
Luzio, Juan Durán. "Bartolomé de las Casas y Michel de Montaigne." In *Bartolomé de las Casas ante la conquista de América,* 223–85. Heredia, Costa Rica: Editorial de la Universidad Nacional, 1992.
Maalouf, Amin. *In the Name of Identity: Violence and the Need to Belong.* New York: Arcade, 2000.
Mahn-Lot, Marianne. *Bartolomé de las Casas et le droit des indiens.* Paris: Payot, 1982.
Majid, Anouar. *A Call for Heresy: Why Dissent Is Vital to Islam and America.* Minneapolis: University of Minnesota Press, 2007.

Bibliography

———. *Freedom and Orthodoxy: Islam and Difference in the Post-Andalusian Age.* Stanford: Stanford University Press, 2004.

———. *Unveiling Traditions: Postcolonial Islam in a Polycentric World.* Durham, NC: Duke University Press, 2000.

Maravall, José Antonio. "Utopía y primitivismo en Las Casas." *Revista de Occidente* 141 (1974) 311–88.

Marchadour, Alain, and David Neuhaus. *The Land, the Bible, and History: Toward The Land That I Will Show You.* New York: Fordham University Press, 2007.

Marcuse, Herbert. *An Essay on Liberation.* Boston, Beacon, 1969.

Martí, José. *Inside the Monster: Writings on the United States and American Imperialism.* New York: Monthly Review, 1975.

———. *Obras escogidas.* La Habana: Editora Política, 1982.

Martínez, Manuel María. "Las Casas-Vitoria y la bula *Sublimis Deus*." In *Estudios sobre Fray Bartolomé de Las Casas*, by André Saint-Lu et al., 25–51. Sevilla: Universidad de Sevilla, 1974.

Martyr of Anghiera, Peter. *De orbe novo.* 2 vols. Edited by Francis Augustus MacNutt. New York: Burt Franklyn, 1970.

Masalha, Nur. *The Bible and Zionism: Invented Traditions, Archaeology and Post-colonialism in Palestine-Israel.* London: Zed, 2007.

———. *Expulsion of the Palestinians: The Concept of "Transfer" in Zionist Political Thought, 1882–1948.* Washington, DC: Institute for Palestine Studies, 1992.

Memmi, Albert. *The Colonizer and the Colonized.* Boston: Beacon, 1965.

Metz, Johannes Baptist. *Zur Theologie der Welt.* Mainz: Matthias-Grúnewald, 1968.

Metzler, Josef. *America Pontificia. Primi saeculi evangelizationis, 1493–1592 documenta Pontificia ex registris et minutis praesertim in archivo secreto Vaticano existentibus, collegit et edidit Josef Metzler.* Vatican City: Librería Editrice Vaticana, 1991.

Mignolo, Walter D. *The Darker Side of the Renaissance: Literacy, Territoriality, & Colonization.* Ann Arbor: The University of Michigan Press, 1995.

———. *The Darker Side of Western Modernity: Global Futures, Decolonial Options.* Durham, NC: Duke University Press, 2011.

———. *Local Histories/Global Designs: Coloniality, Subaltern Knowledges, and Border Thinking.* Princeton: Princeton University Press, 2000.

Milanovic, Branko. "Global Inequality and the Global Inequality Extraction Ratio: The Story of the Past Two Centuries." The World Bank, Development Research Group, Poverty and Inequality Group, September 2009.

Miles, Nelson A. *Serving the Republic: Memoirs of the Civil and Military Life of Nelson A. Miles, Lieutenant-General, United States Army.* New York: Harper, 1911.

Miller, Stuart Creighton. *The Unwelcome Immigrant: The American Image of the Chinese, 1775–1882.* Berkeley: University of California Press, 1969.

Min, Pyong Gap, ed. *Encyclopedia of Racism in the United States.* 3 vols. Westport, CT: Greenwood, 2005.

Miranda, José Porfirio. *Marx y la Biblia.* Salamanca: Sígueme, 1972.

Moltmann, Jürgen. *Theologie der Hoffnung.* München: Chr. Kaiser, 1966.

Montaigne, Michel de. *Essais.* Paris: Imprimerie Nationale, 1998.

Montefiore, Simon Sebag. *Jerusalem: The Biography.* London: Weidenfeld & Nicolson, 2011.

Morales Padrón, Francisco. "Descubrimiento y toma de posesión." *Anuario de estudios americanos* 12, Sevilla (1955) 321–80.

Bibliography

Moore, Stephen D., and Fernando Segovia, eds. *Postcolonial Biblical Criticism: Interdisciplinary Intersections*. London: T. & T. Clark, 2005.
Mostov, Julie. "'Our Women'/'Their Women': Symbolic Boundaries, Territorial Markers, and Violence in the Balkans." *Peace & Change* 20.4 (1995) 515–29.
Motolinia, Toribio de Benavente. *Historia de los indios de la Nueva España: Relación de los ritos antiguos, idolatrías y sacrificios de los indios de la Nueva España, y de la maravillosa conversión que Dios en ella ha obrado*. Edited by Edmundo O'Gorman. México, DF: Porrúa, 1984.
Musicant, Ivan. *Empire By Default: The Spanish-American War and the Dawn of the American Century*. New York: Henry Holt, 1998.
Naipaul, V. S. *The Enigma of Arrival*. Knopf, 1987.
———. *The Mimic Men*. New York, Macmillan, 1967.
Neely, Alan P. "Protestant Antecedents of the Latin American Theology of Liberation." PhD diss., American University, 1977.
Niebuhr, Reinhold. *Moral Man and Immoral Society: A Study in Ethics and Politics*. New York: Scribner's, 1932.
O'Gorman, Edmundo. *La idea del descubrimiento de América: Historia de esa interpretación y crítica de sus fundamentos*. México, DF: Centro de Estudios Filosóficos, 1951.
———. *The Invention of America: An Inquiry into the Historical Nature of the New World and the Meaning of its History*. Bloomington: Indiana University Press 1961.
Oliván, Fernando. *El extranjero y su sombra. Crítica del nacionalismo desde el derecho de extranjería*. Madrid: San Pablo, 1998.
Oren, Michael B. *Six Days of War: June 1967 and the Making of the Modern Middle East*. Oxford: Oxford University Press, 2002.
Ortiz, Fernando. "La leyenda negra contra fray Bartolomé de las Casas." *Cuadernos americanos* 5 (1952) 146–84; 217, 2 (1978) 84–116.
Oviedo y Valdés, Gonzalo Fernández de. *Historia general y natural de las Indias, islas y tierra firme del mar Océano* (1535, 1547). Madrid: Atlas, 1959.
Pagels, Elaine. *The Origin of Satan*. New York: Random House, 1995.
Pagden, Anthony. *The Fall of Natural Man: The American Indian and the Origins of Comparative Ethnology*. Cambridge: Cambridge University Press, 1982.
———. *Lords of all the World: Ideologies of Empire in Spain, Britain and France, c.1500—c.1800*. New Haven: Yale University Press, 1995.
———. *Spanish Imperialism and the Political Imagination*. New Haven: Yale University Press, 1990.
Pappe, Ilan. *The Ethnic Cleansing of Palestine*. Oxford: Oneworld, 2006.
———. *A History of Modern Palestine: One Land, Two Peoples*. Cambridge: Cambridge University Press, 2006.
———. *Out of Frame: The Struggle for Academic Freedom in Israel*. London: Pluto, 2010.
Parish, Helen Rand. *Las Casas en México*. México, DF Fondo de Cultura Económica, 1992.
Pascual Morán, Anaida. *Acción civil noviolenta: fuerza de espíritu, fuerza de paz*. Río Piedras, Puerto Rico: Puertorriqueñas, 2003.
Pérez de Tudela Bueso, Juan, ed. *Obras escogidas de Fray Bartolomé de las Casas, Vol. V: Opúsculos, cartas y memoriales*. Atlas, 1958.
Pérez Fernández, Isacio, O.P. *Cronología documentada de los viajes, estancias y actuaciones de Fray Bartolomé de las Casas*. Bayamón, Puerto Rico: CEDOC, 1983.
———. "La fidelidad del Padre Las Casas a su carisma profético." *Studium*, 16 (1976) 65–109.

Bibliography

———. *Inventario documentado de los escritos de Fray Bartolomé de las Casas.* Bayamón, Puerto Rico: CEDOC, 1981.

———. "El perfil profético del padre Las Casas." *Studium* 15 (1975) 281–359.

Phan, Peter. "Migration in the Patristic Age." In *A Promised Land, A Perilous Journey: Theological Perspectives on Migration*, edited by Daniel G. Groody and Gioacchino Campese, 35–61. Notre Dame, IN: University of Notre Dame Press, 2008.

Phelan, John Leddy. *The Millennial Kingdom of the Franciscans in the New World.* Berkeley: University of California Press, 1956.

Pieris, Aloysius. *An Asian Theology of Liberation.* Maryknoll, NY: Orbis, 1988.

Pimentel Chacón, Jonathan. *Modelos de Dios en las teologías latinoamericanas.* Heredia, Costa Rica: Universidad Nacional de Costa Rica, 2008.

Piterberg, Gabriel. *The Returns of Zionism: Myths, Politics and Scholarship in Israel.* London: Verso, 2008.

Pixley, Jorge V. *Biblia, teología de la liberación y filosofía procesual: el Dios liberador en la Biblia.* Quito, Ecuador: Editorial Abya Yala, 2009.

———. *Exodo, una lectura evangélica y popular.* México, DF: Casa Unida, 1983.

———. *On Exodus: A Liberation Perspective.* Maryknoll, NY: Orbis, 1987.

Pixley Jorge V., and Jean-Pierre Bastian, editors. *Praxis cristiana y producción teológica.* Salamanca: Ediciones Sígueme, 1979.

Pixley, Jorge, et al. *Por un mundo otro: alternativas al mercado global.* Quito, Ecuador: Consejo Latinoamericano de Iglesias, 2003.

Portes, Alejandro and Rubén G. Rumbaut. *Immigrant America: A Portrait* (third edition revised, expanded and updated). Berkeley, CA: University of California Press, 2006.

Posse, Abel. *Los perros del paraíso.* Barcelona: Plaza & Janes Editores, 1987.

Potok, Mark. "Rage in the Right." *Intelligence Report*, Southern Poverty Law Center (Spring 2010) 137 (accessed in www.splcenter.org/get-informed/intelligence-report/browse-all-issues/2010/spring/rage-on-the-right).

Prior, Michael. *The Bible and Colonialism: A Moral Critique.* Sheffield, England: Sheffield Academic, 1997.

———. "Confronting the Bible's Ethnic Cleansing In Palestine." *The Link* (Americans for Middle East Understanding) 33.5 (2000) 1–12.

———. *Jesus the Liberator: Nazareth Liberation Theology (Luke 4. 16–30).* Sheffield, England: Sheffield Academic, 1995.

———. *A Living Stone: Selected Essays & Addresses* by Michael Prior, edited by Duncan Macpherson. London: Living Stones of the Holy Land Trust and Melisende, 2006.

———. *Zionism and the State of Israel: A Moral Inquiry.* London: Routledge, 1999.

Quenum, Alphonse. *Les Églises chrétiennes et la traite atlantique du XVe au XIXe siècle.* Paris: Éditions Karthala, 1993.

Quijano, Aníbal. "Colonialidad del poder, cultura y conocimiento en América Latina." *Anuario Mariateguiano* 9.9 (1998) 113–21.

———. "The Colonial Nature of Power and Latin America's Cultural Experience." In *Sociology in Latin America (Social Knowledge: Heritage, Challenges, Perspectives)*, Proceedings of the Regional Conference of the International Association of Sociology, edited by R. Briceño & H. R. Sonntag, 27–38. Caracas, 1998.

———. "Coloniality of Power, Eurocentrism, and Latin America." *Nepantla* 3 (2000) 533–80.

Quiroga, Vasco de. *Información en derecho* (1535). Introduction and notes by Carlos Herrejón. México, DF: Secretaría de Educación Pública, 1985.

Raboteau, Albert. *A Fire in the Bones: Reflections on African-American Religious History*. Boston: Beacon, 1995.

———. *Slave Religion: The "Invisible Institution" in the Antebellum South*. Oxford: Oxford University Press, 1978.

Raheb, Mitri, ed. *The Biblical text in the Context of Occupation: Towards a New Hermeneutics of Liberation*. Bethlehem, Palestine: Diyar, 2012.

———. *I Am a Palestinian Christian*. Minneapolis: Fortress, 1995.

Ramírez Kidd, José E. *Alterity and Identity in Israel: The "ger" in the Old Testament*. Berlin: De Gruyter, 1999.

Ramos Pérez, Demetrio "La 'conversión' de Las Casas en Cuba: El clérigo y Diego Velázquez." En André Saint-Lu et al., *Estudios sobre Fray Bartolomé de Las Casas*, 247–57. Sevilla: Universidad de Sevilla, 1974.

Ratha, Dilip. "Dollars Without Borders: Can the Global Flow of Remittances Survive the Crisis?" *Foreign Affairs*. (October 16, 2009). Accessed at http://www.foreignaffairs.com/articles/65448/dilip-ratha/dollars-without-borders.

Rech, Bruno. "Bartolomé de las Casas und Aristoteles." *Jahrbuch für Geschichte von Staat, Wirtschaft und Gesellschaft Lateinamerikas* 22 (1985) 39–68.

———. "Las Casas und die Kirchenväter." *Jahrbuch für Geschichte von Staat, Wirtschaft und Gesellschaft Lateinamerikas* 17 (1980) 26–43.

Remesal, Antonio de. *Historia general de las Indias Occidentales y particular de la gobernación de Chiapa y Guatemala*. Guatemala: José de Pineda Ibarra, 1966.

The Revised English Bible, with the Apocrypha. Oxford University Press and Cambridge University Press, 1989.

Ricard, Robert. *The Spiritual Conquest of Mexico: An Essay on the Apostolate and the Evangelizing Methods of the Mendicant Orders in New Spain, 1523–1572*. Translated by Lesley Byrd Simpson. Berkeley: University of California Press, 1966.

Rich, Adrienne. *Poems: Selected and New, 1950–1974*. New York: Norton, 1975.

Richard, Pablo. *Apocalipsis: reconstrucción de la esperanza*. San José: DEI, 1994.

Rieger, Joerg. *Christ & Empire: From Paul to Postcolonial Times*. Minneapolis, MN: Fortress, 2007.

———. "Liberating God-Talk: Postcolonialism and the Challenge of the Margins." In *Postcolonial Theologies: Divinity and Empire*, edited by Catherine Keller, Michael Nausner, and Mayra Rivera, 204–20. St. Louis: Chalice, 2004.

Ríos-Avila, Rubén. "Caribbean Dislocations: Arenas and Ramos Otero in New York." In *Hispanisms and Homosexualities*, edited by Sylvia Molloy and Robert M. Irwin, 101–22. Durham, NC: Duke University Press, 1998.

Rivera, Mayra. "God at the Crossroads: A postcolonial Reading of Sophia." In *Postcolonial Theologies: Divinity and Empire*, edited by Catherine Keller, Michael Nausner, and Mayra Rivera, 186–203. St. Louis, MO: Chalice, 2004.

———. *The Touch of Transcendence: A Postcolonial Theology of God*. Louisville: Westminster John Knox, 2007.

Rivera-Pagán, Luis N. "Bartolomé de las Casas y la esclavitud africana." En Luis N. Rivera-Pagán. *Ensayos teológicos desde el Caribe*, 83–110. San Juan, Puerto Rico: Ediciones Callejón, 2013.

———. "Las Capitulaciones de Burgos: Paradigma de las paradojas de la cristiandad colonial." In *Entre el oro y la fe: El dilema de América*, by Luis N. Rivera-Pagán, 33–60. San Juan, Puerto Rico: Editorial de la Universidad de Puerto Rico, 1995.

———. "Desafíos teológicos del conflicto palestino-israelí," *Signos de Vida* 55 (2010) 6–9.

Bibliography

———. "Doing Pastoral Theology in a Post-Colonial Context: Some Observations from the Caribbean." *Journal of Pastoral Theology* 17.2 (2007) 1–28.

———. *Ensayos teológicos desde el Caribe*. San Juan, Puerto Rico: Ediciones Callejón, 2013.

———. *Entre el oro y la fe: El dilema de América*. San Juan: Editorial de la Universidad de Puerto Rico, 1995.

———. *Essays From the Diaspora*. México, DF: Centro Luterano de Formación Teológica, Publicaciones El Faro, Lutheran School of Theology at Chicago, Centro Basilea de Investigación, 2002.

———. *La evangelización de los pueblos americanos: algunas reflexiones históricas*. San Luis de Potosí, México: Colegio de San Luis, 1997.

———. "Freedom and Servitude: indigenous Slavery in the Spanish Conquest of the Caribbean." In *General History of the Caribbean. Volume I: Autochthonous Societies*, edited by Jalil Sued-Badillo, 316–62. London: UNESCO and Macmillan, 2003.

———. "Iglesia y colonialidad: Tragedia indígena, voz profética y episcopado." In *Ensayos teológicos desde el Caribe*, by Luis N. Rivera-Pagán, 15–45. San Juan, Puerto Rico: Ediciones Callejón, 2013.

———. "Prophecy and Patriotism: A Tragic Dilemma From the Cross of Terror." In *Surviving Terror: Hope and Justice in a World of Violence*, edited by Victoria Erickson and Michelle Lim Jones, 87–101, 315–17. Grand Rapids: Brazos, 2002.

———. "Qui est l'Indien? Humanité ou bestialité de l'indigène américain." *Alternatives Sud. L'avenir des peuples autochtones: Le sort des "premières nations"* vii.2 (2000) 33–51. Centre Tricontinental, Louvain-laNeuve, Belgium.

———. "Religion, War and Peace: Towards an Emancipatory Palestinian Theology." In *Violence, Non-Violence and Religion* (Third International Conference on Christian-Muslim Relations), edited by Fr. Jamal Khader and Angela Hawash-Abu Eita, 169–88, 169–88. Bethlehem: Bethlehem University, Department of Religious Studies, 2011.

———. "For Times Such As This. Oscar Romero: Bishop, Prophet, Martyr." In Luis N. Rivera-Pagean, *Essays From the Diaspora*. México, DF: Centro Luterano de Formación Teológica, Publicaciones El Faro, Lutheran School of Theology at Chicago, Centro Basilea de Investigación, 2002, 89–107.

———. "Toward an Emancipatory Palestinian Theology: Hermeneutical Paradigms and Horizons." In *The Biblical text in the Context of Occupation: Towards a New Hermeneutics of Liberation*, edited by Mitri Raheb, 89–117, 399–408. Bethlehem, Palestine: Diyar, 2012.

———. "Violence of the Conquistadores and Prophetic Indignation." In *Must Christianity Be Violent? Reflections on History, Practice, and Theology*, edited by Kenneth R. Chase & Alan Jacobs, 37–49, 239–43. Grand Rapids: Brazos, 2003.

———. *A Violent Evangelism: The Political and Religious Conquest of the Americas*. Louisville: Westminster John Knox, 1992.

Rodríguez, Jeanette. *Our Lady of Guadalupe: Faith and Empowerment Among Mexican-American Women*. Austin: University of Texas Press, 1994.

Rodríguez, Richard. *Brown: The Last Discovery of America*. New York: Viking, 2002.

Romero, Oscar Romero. *Voice of the Voiceless: The Four Pastoral Letters and other Statements*. Introductory essays by Ignacio Martín-Baró and Jon Sobrino. Maryknoll, NY: Orbis, 1998.

Rosner, Enrique. *Missionare und Musketen: 500 Jahre lateinamerikanische Passion.* Frankfurt am Main: Josef Knecht, 1992.

Ruether, Rosemary Radford. *Faith and Fratricide: The Theological Roots of Anti-Semitism.* New York: Seabury, 1974.

Ruether, Rosemary Radford, and Herman J. Ruether, *The Wrath of Jonah: The Crisis of Religious Nationalism in the Israeli-Palestinian Conflict.* Minneapolis: Fortress, 2002.

Russell, Letty. *Human Liberation in a Feminist Perspective: A Theology.* Philadelphia: Westminster, 1974.

Saadawi, Nawal El. *The Fall of the Imam.* London: Saqi, 2002.

———. *Walking Through Fire: A Life of Nawal El Saadawi.* London and New York: Zed, 2003.

Sacks, Jonathan. *The Dignity of Difference: How to Avoid the Clash of Civilizations.* London: Continuum, 2003.

Said, Edward. *Culture and Imperialism.* New York: Knopf, 1993.

———. *Freud and the Non-European.* London: Verso, 2003.

———. "Michael Walzer's 'Exodus and Revolution': A Canaanite Reading." *Grand Street*, 5.2 (Winter 1986) 86–106.

———. *Out of Place: A Memoir.* New York: Knopf, 1999.

———. *Orientalism.* 25th anniversary edition. New York: Random House, 2003.

———. *The Question of Palestine.* London: Routledge, 1980.

———. *Reflections on Exile and Other Essays.* Cambridge: Harvard University Press, 2002.

———. *Representations of the Intellectuals.* New York: Vintage, 1996.

Sand, Shlomo. *The Invention of the Jewish People.* New York: Verso, 2009.

Sanneh, Lamin. *Translating the Message: The Missionary Impact on Culture.* Maryknoll, NY: Orbis, 1989.

Sartori, Giovanni. *Pluralismo, multiculturalismo e estranei: saggio sulla società multietnica.* Milano: Rizzoli, 2000.

Schüssler Fiorenza, Elisabeth. *Changing Horizons: Explorations in Feminist Interpretation.* Minneapolis: Fortress, 2013.

———. "Feminist Theology as a Critical Theology of Liberation." *Theological Studies* 36 (1975) 605–26.

———. *In Memory of Her: A Feminist Theological Reconstruction of Christian Origins.* New York: Crossroad, 1994.

Schwartz, Regina M. *The Curse of Cain: The Violent Legacy of Monotheism.* Chicago and London: University of Chicago Press, 1997.

Schweiker, William. *Theological Ethics and Global Dynamics In the Time of Many Worlds.* Malden, MA: Blackwell, 2004.

Segovia, Fernando. "Mapping the Postcolonial Optic in Biblical Criticism: Meaning and Scope." In *Postcolonial Biblical Criticism: Interdisciplinary Intersections*, edited by Stephen D. Moore, and Fernando Segovia, 23–78. London/New York: T. & T. Clark, 2005.

———. "From 1968, through 2008: A Call to Action for Latino/a American Religious and Theological Studies." *Apuntes* 28.1 (2008) 4–28.

———. "Engaging the Palestinian Theological-Critical Project of Liberation: A Critical Dialogue." In *The Biblical text in the Context of Occupation: Towards a New Hermeneutics of Liberation*, edited by Mitri Raheb, 29–80, 395–99. Bethlehem, Palestine: Diyar, 2012.

Bibliography

Segundo, Juan Luis. *Liberación de la teología*. Buenos Aires: Carlos Lohlé, 1975.
———. *The Liberation of Theology*. Maryknoll, NY: Orbis, 1976.
———. *Teología de la liberación: Respuesta al Cardenal Ratzinger*. Madrid: Ediciones Cristiandad, 1985.
Sepúlveda, Juan Ginés de. *Democrates secundus, sive de iustis belli causis*. Critical edition and translation by A. Coroleu Lletget. In Juan Ginés de Sepúlveda, *Obras completas*, 3:38–134. Pozoblanco: Excmo. Ayuntamiento de Pozoblanco, 1997.
———. "Proposiciones temerarias, escandalosas y heréticas que notó el doctor Sepúlveda en el libro de la conquista de Indias, que fray Bartolomé de las Casas, obispo que fué de Chiapa, hizo imprimir 'sin licencia' en Sevilla, año de 1552, cuyo título comienza: 'Aquí se contiene una disputa o controversia.'" In *Vida y escritos de don Fray Bartolomé de Las Casas, Obispo de Chiapa*, by Antonio María Fabié, 2:543–69. Madrid: Imprenta de Miguel Ginesta, 1879.
Shapira, Anita. *The Bible and Israeli Identity*. Jerusalem: Magnes, 2006.
Shaull, Richard. *Hombre, ideología y revolución en América Latina*. ISAL: Montevideo, 1965.
Shiels, William Eugene, S. I. *King and Church: The Rise and Fall of the Patronato Real*. Chicago: Loyola University Press, 1961.
Silva Gotay, Samuel. *El pensamiento cristiano revolucionario en América Latina y El Caribe: Implicaciones de la teología de la liberación para la sociología de la religión*. Salamanca: Ediciones Sígueme, 1981.
———. *O pensamento cristão revolucionãrio na América Latina e no Caribe (1960–1973)*. São Paulo: Edições Paulinas, 1985.
———. *Christentum und Revolution in Lateinamerika und der Karibik: Die Bedeutung der Theologie der Befreiung für eine Soziologie der Religion*. Frankfurt am Main: Würzburger Studien zur Fundamentaltheologie, Band 17, 1995.
Singer, Isaac Bashevis. *The Penitent*. New York: Farrar, Straus, and Giroux, 1983.
———. *Collected Stories: Gimpel the Fool to The Letter Writer*. New York: The Library of America, 2004.
Sizer, Stephen. *Christian Zionism: Road-map to Armageddon?* Downers Grove, IL: IVO Academic, 2005.
Smith, Robert O. *More Desired than Our Owne Salvation: The Roots of Christian Zionism*. New York: Oxford University Press, 2013.
Smith-Christopher, Daniel L. *A Biblical Theology of Exile*. Minneapolis: Fortress, 2002.
Snyder, Susanna. *Asylum-Seeking, Migration and Church*. Farnham, Surrey, UK: Ashgate, 2012.
Sobrino, Jon. *Jesucristo liberador: lectura histórico teológica de Jesús de Nazaret*. San Salvador: UCA, 1991.
———. *La fe en Jesucristo: ensayo desde las víctimas*. San Salvador: UCA, 1999.
Soerens, Matthew and Jenny Hwang. *Welcoming the Stranger: Justice, Compassion & Truth in the Immigration Debate*. Downers Grove, IL: IVP, 2009.
Sölle, Dorothee. *Politische Theologie. Auseinandersetzung mit Rudolf Bultmann*. Stuttgart: Kreuz-Verlag, 1971.
Sontag, Susan. *Regarding the Pain of Others*. New York: Farrar, Straus and Giroux, 2003.
Spivak, Gayatri Chakravorty. *In Other Worlds: Essays in Cultural Politics*. New York: Routledge, 1998.

———. "Can the Subaltern Speak?" In *Marxism and the Interpretation of Culture*, edited by Cary Nelson and Lawrence Grossberg, 271–313. Urbana: University of Illinois Press, 1988.
Stalker, Peter. *Workers Without Frontiers: The Impact of Globalization on International Migration*. Geneva: International Labor Organization, 2000.
Steiner, George. "Our Homeland, the Text." In *No Passion Spent: Essays 1978–1996*, 304–27. London: Faber, 1996.
Stuart, Elizabeth. *Gay and Lesbian Theologies: Repetitions with Critical Difference*. Burlington, VT: Ashgate, 2003.
Styron, William. *Darkness Visible: A Memoir of Madness*. New York: Random House, 1990.
Sued Badillo, Jalil. "Christopher Columbus and the Enslavement of Amerindians in the Caribbean." *Monthly Review* 44.3 (1992) 71–102.
Sugirtharajah, R. S., editor. *The Postcolonial Bible*. Sheffield, England: Sheffield Academic, 1998.
———. "Complacencies and Cul-de-sacs: Christian Theologies and Colonialism." In *Postcolonial Theologies: Divinity and Empire*, edited by Catherine Keller, Michael Nausner, and Mayra Rivera, 22–38. St. Louis: Chalice, 2004.
———. *The Postcolonial Biblical Reader*. Malden, MA and Oxford: Blackwell, 2006.
———. *Postcolonial Criticism and Biblical Interpretation*. Oxford: Oxford University Press, 2002.
Taylor, Mark Lewis. *Religion, Politics, and the Christian Right: Post-9/11 Powers and American Empire*. Minneapolis: Fortress, 2005.
Tertullian. "On the Apparel of Women." In *The Ante-Nicene Fathers: Vol IV*, edited by Alexander Roberts and James Donaldson, 14–26. Grand Rapids: Eerdmans, 1965.
Thacher, John Boyd. *Christopher Columbus: His Life, His Work, His Remains*. New York: Kraus, 1967, orig. 1903–1904.
Tinker, George E. *Spirit and Resistance: Political Theology and American Indian Liberation*. Minneapolis: Fortress, 2004.
Tocqueville, Alexis de. *Democracy in America*. London: Oxford University Press, 1959.
Tordesillas, Antonio de Herrera y. *Historia general de los hechos de los castellanos en las islas y tierra firme del Mar Océano* (1601–1605). Madrid: Real Academia de la Historia, 1934–1957.
Trías Monge, José. *Puerto Rico: The Trials of the Oldest Colony in the World*. New Haven: Yale University Press, 1997.
Trible, Phyllis. *God and the Rhetoric of Sexuality*. Philadelphia: Fortress, 1978.
———. *Texts of Terror: Literary-Feminist Readings of Biblical Narratives*. Philadelphia: Fortress, 1984.
Trouillot, Michel-Rolph. *Silencing the Past: Power and the Production of History*. Boston: Beacon, 1995.
Valentin, Benjamin. *Mapping Public Theology: Beyond Culture, Identity, and Difference*. Harrisburg/London: Trinity Press International, 2002.
Vespucio, Américo. *El Nuevo Mundo, cartas relativas a sus viajes y descubrimientos* (textos en italiano, español e inglés, estudio preliminar de Roberto. Levillier). Buenos Aires: Nova, 1951.
Vigil, José María, editor. *Bajar de la Cruz a los Pobres: Cristología de la Liberación*. México, DF: Dabar, 2007.
Vitoria, Francisco de. *Obras de Francisco de Vitoria: Relecciones teológicas*. Critical edition of the Latin text, Spanish version, general introduction and introductions with

Bibliography

the study of his theological-juridical doctrine by Teófilo Urdanoz, O.P. Madrid: Biblioteca de Autores Cristianos, 1960.

———. *Political Writings*. Edited by Anthony Pagden and Jeremy Lawrance. Cambridge: Cambridge University Press, 1996.

Volf, Miroslav. *Exclusion and Embrace: A Theological Exploration of Identity, Otherness, and Reconciliation*. Nashville: Abingdon, 1996.

Walcott, Derek. "The Schooner 'Flight.'" In *Collected Poems, 1948–1984*, 345–61. New York: Farrar, Straus and Giroux, 1986.

Walker, Alice. "Overcoming Speechlessness." *Tikkun* (September/October 2009) 35–36.

Walls, Andrew. *The Missionary Movement in Christian History: Studies in the Transmission of Faith*. Maryknoll, NY: Orbis, 2000.

Walzer, Michael. *Exodus and Revolution*. New York: Basic, 1985.

Walzer, Michael, and Edward Said. "An Exchange: 'Exodus and Revolution.'" *Grand Street* 5.4 (Summer 1986) 246–59.

Wagner, Henry Raup, with the collaboration of Helen Rand Parish. *The Life and Writings of Bartolomé de las Casas*. Albuquerque: University of New Mexico Press, 1967.

Weil, Simone. "*L'Iliade* ou le poème de la force." *Oeuvres complètes*. Paris: Gallimard, 1989.

———. "Reflection's on War." In *Formative Writings, 1929–1941*, edited and translated by Dorothy Tuck McFarland and Wilhelmina Van Ness, 237–48. Amherst: The University of Massachusetts Press, 1987.

———. "The *Iliad*, Poem of Might." In *The Simone Weil Reader*, edited by George A. Panichas, 153–83. New York: David McKay, 1977.

———. "The Love of God and Affliction." In *The Simone Weil Reader*, edited by George A. Panichas, 439–468. New York: David McKay Co., 1977.

West, Cornel. *Democracy Matters: Winning the Fight Against Imperialism*. New York: Penguin, 2004.

Whitelam, Keith W. *The Invention of Ancient Israel: The Silencing of Palestinian History*. London/New York: Routledge, 1996.

Wilson, Andrew. "Black slaves and messianic dreams in Bartolomé de Las Casas's plans for an abundant Indies." PhD diss., Princeton Theological Seminary, 2009.

Wit, Hans de. *En la dispersión el texto es patria: Introducción a la hermenéutica clásica, moderna y posmoderna*. San José, Costa Rica: Universidad Bíblica Latinoamericana, 2002.

Witte, Charles-Martial de. "Les bulles pontificales et l'expansion portugaise au XVe siècle." *Revue d'histoire ecclésiastique*, 48 (1953) 683–718; 49 (1954) 438–61; 51 (1956) 413–53, 809–36; 53 (1958) 5–46, 443–71.

Yeats, William Butler. "The Second Coming" (1919/1920). In *The New Oxford Book of English Verse, 1250–1950*, edited by Helen Gardner, 820. Oxford: Oxford University Press, 1972.

Yiftachel, Oren. *Ethnocracy: Land and Identity in Israel/Palestine*. Philadelphia: University of Pennsylvania Press, 2006.

Zamora, José A., editor. *Ciudadanía, multiculturalidad e inmigración*. Navarra, España: Verbo Divino, 2003.

Zavala, Silvio A. "¿Las Casas esclavista?" *Cuadernos americanos* 3.2 (1944) 149–54.

www.ingramcontent.com/pod-product-compliance
Lightning Source LLC
Chambersburg PA
CBHW022124160426
43197CB00009B/1140